R 306/15

COOKING One's CORGi

MiKe HARDiNG

COOKING One's CORGi

Robson Books

The publisher acknowledges with thanks, the permission of the *Weekly World News* to reproduce the stories which appear on pages 145 to 157.

First published in Great Britain in 1988 by Robson Books Ltd.
Reprinted October 1988.

Bolsover House, 5-6 Clipstone Street, London W1P 7EB
Copyright © 1988 Mike Harding

British Cataloguing in Publication Data

Harding Mike, 1944-
  Cooking One's Corgi.
  I. Title
ISBN 0 86051 529 X

All rights reserved. No part of this publication may be reproduced, stored in a retrieval system, or transmitted in any form or by any means, electronic, mechanical, photocopying, recording or otherwise, without prior permission in writing of the publishers.

Designed by **Central Station Design**, Manchester.
Typeset by **Jetset,** Manchester.

Printed and bound in Great Britain by Billing and Sons Ltd. Worcester.

MiKe HARDiNG

COOKING One's CORGi

contents

'THIS IS GETTING TO BE A BORE' SAID JIMSOM
'EVERY TIME I RUB THIS PLATE THIS BLOODY
GENI POLICEMAN APPEARS AND OFFFERS ME
A BENT VIDEO!'

'YOU SAID **YOU'D** BRING THE
ROPE' HISSED MORIARTY DESPAIRINGLY

Bunter comes up TRUMPS

A RIPPING YARN OF SCHOOLBOY LIFE

The Fat Owl of the Remove was feeling mossy, definitely mossy. Lying awake in the dorm one night, he heard above the rhythmic sounds of future cabinet ministers buggering each other, a noise at once low and confusing yet ominous. It reminded the poor lard barrel of nothing more than the noise made by that acid stuff when Old Podger poured it on the zinc filings in Stinks.

He reached in his bedside locker for his *Boy's Own Book of Diseases of the Alimentary Tract*. It was under his four ton stack of *Health and Efficiency*.

'I say Bunter! You're not pulling the old pud again are you?' asked Cherry from the next bed.

'Bunter's bashing his bishop!' whooped Jones Minor in a muffled tone, his face in Cherry's pillow.

Bunter ignored them and strapped on his Petzl headtorch.

Under the sheets he scanned the tome. All around him were shouts of 'One off the Wrist! Five fingered widow! Stroking the old sausage eh! Bunter?'

Even Hurree Ram Jam Full, purveyor of quartz digital watches, Marks & Spencer's seconds and cheap personal stereos to Grey friars muttered something about the the Fat Owl 'pulling his popadum'.

After a few minutes an ashen-faced porker raised his head from beneath the sheets, the beam from his head torch flashing across the row of beds opposite where a future High Commissioner to Botswanaland was performing an indiscretion that would cost him his post when discovered practising it in a gents' toilet in Dorking.

'I say you chaps,' croaked the Fat Owl, 'I think I've got an ulcer!'

'Oh the duodenalfulness is terrific!' howled Ram Jam Full in delight.

'I say chaps! What say we go and raid someone's chocolate locker!! What!!' cried Cherry, excitedly punching Jones Minor's freckle.

'Bog off!' muttered Jones Minor, his face in Cherry's pillow.

The next morning at prep in Study No. 1 the chums of the Remove were disturbed in their attempts to roast one of their members alive over the blazing fire in the venerable old inglenook, by the sudden and dramatic entrance of Old Korky their housemaster who had at his side a boy none of them recognised.

They put down the singed scholar and stood in postures of languid attention at their desks.

'This, boys,' said Mr Corkindale, pointing at the stocky figure by his side, 'is Arkwright. His father is manually engaged for

weekly pecuniary reward in the extraction of a carboniferous combustible somewhere in the North in the region of Barnsley and having been successful in that great hope of the plebian masses, the Littlewood's soccer lottery, has decided to send his son here to be couthed. I do hope that in the spirit of Greyfriars and remembering the school motto *'Clavus illes laborares'** you will make him at home.'

And so saying Old Korky about faced and left the study where twelve open-mouthed scions of privilege and prejudice stared at the newcomer.

Cherry was the first to speak.

'I say chaps!' he crowed. 'It's an oik! Let's scrag him!'

'Give him beans!' said Johny Bull.

'The beanfullness is the proper caper!' said Hurree Ram Jam Full.

'Oh my hat,' Cherry ejaculated, picking himself up off the dusty floor with a broken nose and missing front tooth.

After that the chums of the Remove left Arkwright severely alone. They soon got used to his strange habit of keeping coal in the bath and his diet of strong tea and fish and chips and after a few boys had been hospitalised even the most fervent and enthusiastic amorati gave up trying to get into his bed.

But for the most part Arkwright was cut by the chums of the Remove and became a figure of mystery and rumour. Even the Fat Owl gave him a wide berth in spite of the fact that Arkwright received a thousand pounds a week pocket money. But then the Fat Owl had other problems. His ulcer had meant that the matron had put him on a diet of milk and fish and the poor dumpling hated it.

'I say you chaps!' he groaned one morning in prep. 'Lor crikey! I mean it isn't fair! I mean I'd rather be dead than not eat , don't you know! I mean' he screeched 'what's a chap to do if he can't scoff?'

'You could always do what Parkinson did' chuckled Cherry.

Parkinson was a handsome hetero who had got into trouble one of the local girls who worked at Greyfriars as a maid. He had been one of matron's favourites and it had looked for a time as though he was going to get the sack but somehow he had mysteriously reappeared as captain of the first eleven, head boy

*Screw the workers

10

of Filth House and treasurer of the stamp club.

The Fat Boy thought of Parkinson and sex, something that the Owl had always seen as too bumpy and energetic for words, and stared at the mush of cod and milk before him.

'Oh Lawks! Lumme!' he muttered despairingly.

On Founder's Day, Greyfriars School held its annual cross-country run, a hard slog of twelve miles across some of the roughest and hardest country for miles. Some of the hills were thirty foot high and there were raging streams almost three feet wide across which one had to leap. All the weeds, wets and milksops of the school dreaded it. It was a sport Cherry excelled in and he always finished way ahead of the rest of the school, even having enough time to bugger a few locals on his way round.

The Fat Owl waddled out of Shell on the morning of the race, whining and moaning.

'I say you chaps I mean crikey! What! I mean I could die! I mean – oh lor! lumme! It's my ulcer don't you know. I say Ouch! Yarooh!!!'

But all was to no avail and garbed in a pair of shorts that would have made a tent for a family of Lapps and a vest that stretched across his broad acres like a Christo sculpture, the mountain of lard plodded his thunderous way through the gates of that most venerable of old piles already half an hour behind the slowest of the pack (including Morgan whose legs were in plaster as a result of his defaulting on his protection money and who was being carried over the course by matron - for a fee).

In the far distance the Fat Owl could see the specks of humanity that were the boys of Greyfriars, England's hopes for the future, scudding over the historic chalk slopes of what Shakespeare once called *'This Septic Isle'*. After half a mile or so, his heart beating like a jungle drum, the Great Blob flopped down on the grass in the sunshine gasping for air like a stranded whale.

When he had recovered enough to be conscious of things about him, his hearing told him that he was not entirely alone. Coming

from a shallow defile that was cloaked in bushes the Fat Owl could hear sounds of giggling and merriment, and what's more, the poor blimp could **smell food!!!**

Rolling stealthily towards the sound on his ample tum, like a bespectacled slug in shorts and vest the Paunchy Porker parted the privets and peered through the gap.

What he saw amazed him for there was Arkwright stark naked, a blonde on one side and a red head on the other - both similarly clothed. They and Arkwright were kissing and touching each others' cheeky bits and doing other things too rude to mention.

But the Obese Owl was oblivious to this, for spread on the grassy knoll before them was a mountain of grub. Such grub as the Fat Boy only dreamed of in his wildest dreams! Three hundred steak and kidney pies, ten gallons of mushy peas, a quart of extra strong spicy pickled onions and a firkin of Marston's Pedigree Ale!!!! The Great Gasbag's greedy eyes glistened.

'!!!!Oh Lawks! Crikey! I mean! Oh I say! I mean! I mean! Oh Lawks! Oh Lumme! TUCK TUCK TUCK!!! And the Lumpy Lardbarrel slithered down the slope to come to rest panting breathlessly before the naked trio.

'You ought to wash yer mouth out!!' said one of the girls who was a little hard of hearing.

'Ey up! Sithee! It's Bunter!' said Arkwright laughingly. 'Aye there's lots of snap tha knows, Bunter. Help theesen! I never could bonk on an empty stomach an' I likes ter mek sure me tarts are tret well too.'

But the Fat Owl had heard nothing at all after the words *'help theesen'* and had scoffed four pies, a bowlful of mushy peas with half a dozen pickles and washed it down with a pint and a half of ale before Arkwright had finished talking.

Two hours later the Great Blimp was helpless on his back, all round him crumbs and empty pie cases, the barrel almost drained to the dregs.

'Oh Lor!! Crumbs!! Crikey (*burp!!! belch!!! boop!!! whizz!!!!*) I mean Yarooh!! Oh Lawks!! There's going to be an awful scragging! I mean the rest of the chaps must all be finished by now. We shall be whacked!!!! Oh Lawks! Ouch! Yarooh!!!' and he yelped in anticipation of the whacking he was surely going to get.

'Nay tha great Pillock! Tha'll not get belted. Tha knows ah knows a short cut. Dahn theer in t'bushes there's one of the owd

smugglers' secret passageways. If tha teks that, tha comes dahn to t'sea and then if tha cuts back in under t'cliff through another passageway tha comes out reet by t'finishin line tha knows!

'Come on ah'll come wi' thee!! Thee clear up girls an' ah'll sithee in t'boozer terneet!!! Here y'are 'ave a 'undred pound each ter buy some sexy undies!!' and he thrust the notes at them, hurriedly pulling on his shorts and vest and leading the Fat Owl through the bushes.

There before them was a round tunnel mouth, the entrance to a secret passageway. They entered. After plodding down the passage for a couple of hundred yards they heard ahead of them the sound of the sea.

'We're nearly there Owd Tub,' said Arkwright.

'I say Arkwright,' croaked the Fat Owl, 'I know that the rest of the chaps don't like you much, what with you being working class and that. But I think you're a brick – put it there what!' and he held out a podgy flipper. Arkwright shook it.

'And thou aren't as stuck up as t'other toffee-nosed snobs either Bunter.'

Suddenly they heard voices coming from the daylight at the end of the tunnel – German voices!!!

'Howd thy noise!!' hissed Arkwright, creeping stealthily forward.

The two chums peered out of the tunnel mouth. Ahead of them was the narrow little bay with its high cliffs and shingle beach. Pulling a rubber dinghy up the shingle were six men while riding at sea, not a hundred yards away, was a German submarine.

One of the men had boots and a uniform on.

'That'll be the captain of the U-boat,' whispered Bunter. Two of the other men had white sweaters and cropped hair. 'They're sailors from the submarine and they've rowed the others ashore,' hissed the Owl rubbing his glasses with his finger and thumb, 'the other three are German spies.'

'What are we gooin' ter doo!' asked Arkwight. Ah can feet four on 'em but six is a bit much!!'

'Leave it to me,' said the Owl, and striding from the tunnel onto the beach he cried, 'I arrest you in the name of His Majesty's Government as spies and saboteurs. You had better come quietly or I will be forced to shoot.'

The Germans laughed uproariously – even those who didn't understand English.

'Oh das is zo gut!!!' shrieked the Captain helplessly. 'Ze fat boy is arrestink us! Ho! Mein Gott in Himmel! Ho! Ho! Ho! Qvick Kurt kill zem both! Ho! Ho! Ho!'

At his orders one of the ratings levelled a Mauser at the two chums.

'You asked for it you damn Krauts!!' squeaked the Fat Boy. And bending over with his back to them, full to the tonsils with ale, pickles and mushy peas, the Fat Owl let fly the most enormous fart that instantly killed Kurt, blinding the Captain, concussing the spies and sinking the submarine with the loss of all hands.

Tying them up with the shreds of his blown apart shorts, Bunter sat on the ugliest of the spies killing him slightly.

'Arkwright,' he commanded, 'you go back to the school and tell the Head to send the police and the local militia. I'll keep guard over this lot.' And picking up a bratwurst and a bottle of German beer from a hamper that stood on the beach he commenced tucking into the spread.

'Not as good as our English tuck don't you know but it'll stave off the hunger pangs till tea time.'

And off Arkwright sped muttering, 'Well ah'll be buggered' which was not quite true.

With the police and the army came Mr Coldshower the sports master and half the boys in the school whooping and yelling.

'Well done Bunter you're a brick,' chortled Mr Coldshower.

'Three cheers for the Fat Owl!!' he called and the cliffs of the Bay rang to the sound of sturdy young English voices.

Arkwright was borne aloft back to Greyfriars on the shoulders of the chums while Bunter was pushed in a wheelbarrow.

Later that evening at a giant feast in his honour given by the school it was learnt that the Germans were actually Martians planning to destroy the world and that Bunter had saved the Universe from extinction.

'Bunter and Arkwright, we have sadly misjudged you both,' said the Head cringingly. 'I am now going away to drink vitriol

but in the meantime here is a Toff from the Government to speak to you.'

And a fat man with diamond studded rings and a cigar swept into the room.

'Well done Bunter!' said the Toff from the Government. 'And

there's more good news to come. A Harley Street surgeon is coming to the school tomorrow and he's going to give you a new body.'

'Oh Lawks!! Crikey! I mean . . .' stammered the Fat Boy, for once lost for words. 'In that case sir I'll have Cherry's body – er – if you don't mind that is – sir!!'

There were cheers all round the Great Hall.

'It shall be done' beamed the Toff and, turning to them both he added, 'and here's a million pounds each from a grateful King and Country.'

'Hurrah !!' cried the school.

'Swoon !!!' said the two chums.

THE END

NEXT WEEK: *BUNTER AND THE TREASURE OF THE SIERRA MADRE* PLUS A FREE JOKE EXPLODING CONDOM FOR ALL OUR READERS!!!

QUICK! RUN AND GET YOUR GUITARS –
ANDY KERSHAW'S COMING!

'EUREKA!!'
SHRIEKED THOMPSON
THE INVENTOR OF
THE LUMINOUS CONDOM!
NO MORE FUMBLING
IN THE DARK!

A DAY OUT AT SELLAFIELD – VISITING
THE CONTROL ROOM

A BEGINNER'S GUIDE TO THE ENGLISH LANGUAGE

THE ORIGINS OF THE SPEECHES

Prior to the invention of Language by Eric the Gob, Mankind spoke in a series of quacking sounds that had been learnt from the first animals Man came into contact with – the giant meat-eating Ducks of the Olduvai Gorge in what is now Africa but was then Kidderminster.

For centuries after leaving the Garden of Eden, Man quacked his way around the globe until he got fed up with God throwing stale crusts at him and decided to invent language instead.

THE INVENTION OF LANGUAGE

Human language was invented by Eric the Gob as he sat one morning in his cave. It was a dull November day, foggy and cold and wet. The fire had gone out and holes in the roof were letting the rain in. Water was running down the walls making the pictures of the bisons and men with bows and arrows run and go all long and stringy. Two giant mastodons had forced their way into the cave and were sat either side of Eric staring out at the constantly falling rain. A parrot coughed in the coal ferns. Steadily the water dripped onto the cold ashes and what was left of last night's

22

take-away mammoth. All around were the tribe staring glumly out at the wet, grey, miserable, cold, sodden, gloomy day. All of a sudden, out of nowhere came the first words ever uttered by mankind.

'I'm bored,' said Eric who was promptly stoned to death by the rest of the clan.

'I'm bored', said Eric

But not before that word had lodged itself inside the wrinkled cranium of all the Cro-magnons in the cave.

For two hundred thousand years 'Boring' was the only word in the language. It had to stand for a lot of things from beautiful sunsets to violent death, from the colour of a pair of brown shoes to sexual ecstasy.

The second word to come along was 'refrigerator' coined by Eric the Salesman who discovered that keeping a dead mammoth on ice stopped it stinking in hot weather and provided you with mammoth steaks for the barbecue all the year round.

After that the words came thick and thin. Children in particular had trouble with thick words because their mouths were too small and grown-ups often had to chew them up for them first.

DIFFERENT KINDS OF LANGUAGE DEVELOP

Man developed many different kinds of language, from Mandarin Chinese to Eskimo, from Geordie to Aborigine. It is not known why we all speak different languages. One theory is that the Tower of Babel overtime strike resulted in the fragmentation of the unions, closed shops, demarcation disputes and people not speaking to each other. Another theory is that God did it so we would be able to laugh at foreigners.

Another seemingly insoluble mystery is why words are used in a definite order.

? Mean I the, if were order in a words different understand would you them.

The only common point that all languages share is that they all use words, and with the exception of politicians all the sounds employed to make the words are made with the mouth.

THE NOISES WE MAKE

Philologists have examined the sounds that Man makes with his mouth and have been able to tabulate them. The 'f' sound of the word 'father' for example is a labio-dental fricative, because it is made by the teeth and the lips. The 'g' sound used in the word 'god' is a glottal sound but when it's used in the word 'genius' it is an alveolar palatal fricative. The sound 'p' as in 'pod' is a labial plosive.

So now armed with such knowledge you should be able to work out what an 'anal fricative plosive' is.

Your answer should be in not less than two words and should be written on no more than two sides of the paper.

THE SIGNS WE MAKE

Language is more than sounds though. The sounds actually stand for or 'signify' something.

They are symbols of things.

The word 'water' for example is not really water, only a symbol

for it. That is why you can say 'water' as much as you like and yet you'll still die of thirst. Which only proves how bloody useless language is to all intents and purposes.

Raw emotions are conveyed by the most basic sounds and are difficult to capture in writing.

A low moan accompanied by dribbling noises could convey hunger, pain, lust or imminent death. Whereas the words 'You are sacked' are fairly unambiguous.

A low moan accompanied by dribbling noises

THE ENGLISH LANGUAGE

In the beginning in the islands of Britain, everybody, all seven of them including the gran, spoke Early Caveish.

This consisted of a lot of grunts and pointing and basic words like *boring, refrigerator, fire, filofax* and *orgasm.* For us today listening to those sounds it would be hard to tell whether the people were making love, fighting or asking the milkman for an extra bottle of gold top and a carton of Fruits of the Forest yoghurt.

Not long after Early Caveish came Later Caveish distinguished from Early Caveish by the fact that some of the grunts had become more complex words like *value added tax* and *pension fund.* Then somebody on a damp afternoon in one of the Lascaux caves got hacked off with painting sabre-toothed tigers and invented the abstract noun thus bringing into being LOVE, HATE, FEAR, TIME and DEATH.

Until the invention of abstract nouns, the emotions they described were diagnosed as simple cases of acid indigestion ranging from mild in the case of 'Love' to acute in the case of 'Death'.

This, of course, was confusing and many people didn't know whether they were Dead or in Love: and sometimes it was very hard to tell.

THE INVENTION OF BOOKS

The first recorded books were carved on stone in Very Late Caveish and were the Ladybird Early Man Early Reader Series. The books weighed nearly a ton each so that overdue fines at the library on account of hernias, wheels fallen off wagons etc. were very common. The books followed the adventures of two colourless characters called Ug and Ug and contained such wonderful stories as *Ug and Ug Go To The Cave, Ug and Ug discover Fire* and *Ug and Ug get Burnt to Death.*

In the books you find such enchanting little cameos as the following:

See Ug run. See the Dinosaur. See Ug chase the Dinosaur. See Ug has bad eyes. See Ug thinks the dino is daddy. See Ug splattered. See everybody laugh.

The only place where this Early Very Late Caveish language is still spoken is Glasgow. It is still possible 'doon the Barras' to hear phrases such as 'see bevvy, see me, see last night, see wrecked!' and verbs are conjugated thus:

> *see me*
> *see you*
> *see him*
> *see her*
> *see us*
> *see yous*
> *see they bastards*

THE CELTIC INVASION

Not long after Later Caveish came the influx of Celtic into these islands.

Celtic is the sort of language you hear at football matches in Scotland now and it has a few words of Later Caveish in it and a lot of Celtic words about maiming people.

See you pal ahm no kiddin' ah'll rip yer heed aff

Two kinds of Celtic reached these islands brought here respectively by the P Celts and Q Celts.

The P Celts used letter p as per normal while the Q Celts used the letter q where we use p today, e.g.

Qeter qiqer qicked a qeck of qickled qeqqer

Nobody took the Q Celts seriously and they died out with people laughing at them. In fact the only people who speak 'Q – Celtic' today are ventriloquists e.g.

a qint of gitter qlease langlorg.

ROMANS IN THE GLOMAN

Not long after this the Romans invaded and by dastardly deeds were able to drive the Celts westward into the fastnesses of Cornwall, Wales, Cumbria, Scotland and Ireland in which latter place they are still to be found living at the end of rainbows and under stones only coming out to open gates for gentlemen.

The English Celts died out for many reasons:
> (a) *they were too busy laughing at each other's pronunci-ation – hence the expression 'minding one's p's and q's'*
> (b) *they were too busy killing each other*
> (c) *with names like Cogidumnus and Vercengatorix and Caractacus nobody took them seriously anyway*
> (d) *the Romans had a counting system that went up to ten and then increased with units of ten whereas the Celts just had 1, 2 and 3 and after that anything more than three was either **a lot, a bloody lot** or **a bloody piggin' big lot!!***

This made the ordering of supplies for the Celtic armies very difficult. They were either starving and running out of woad or were so full of food and slippery with woad that they couldn't fight.

The Roman language while not superior to Celtic was more suited to conquest, exploitation and soft furnishings.

The Celts for example had no words for hot baths, hypocaust, olive oil, back massage and such phrases as *'do you live with your parents?'*

The Romans brought thousands of words into England during their occupation of the larger of the two islands – they arrived at Dover docks by the crateload every day. In fact the very first recorded strike in British history was the Dover Dock Strike of 64AD when a group of Celts refused to unload some crates of Latin nouns because *'they were too slippery, they smelt of garlic and were in ablative and dative cases when they should have been in sacks'*, as one of them put it.

DOCKERS HOLD COUNTRY TO RANSOM read the headline in the *Sun, Star, Daily Mail* and *Daily Express* for the first but by no means the last time.

A lot of Latin words were left behind after the Romans left. They can still be seen in heaps around the forts of the Saxon shore and are up for grabs if anybody wants them since they're not much use any more. I mean if you said *'Quo Vadis Mater?'* to your mother as she was going out shopping she would probably wash your mouth out with soap and a good thing too.

THE ANGLED SAXONS

After the Romans came the Angled Saxons who arrived with nothing but words with four letters, swear words and words about the damp and interesting bits of the human body or words that were about generally misbehaving.

Bum, bosom, bottom, knockers, fart, drink, drunk, hangover, skinful and *alka-seltzer* are all Anglo Saxon words. In fact the

Anglo Saxon Chronicle, a form of newspaper found on bus shelters and lavatory walls in those days, would make today's *Sun* and *Star* look like hymn sheets. It carried headlines such as **UP YOURS HERGEST** and had a page three girl clad in nothing but a tiny daub of triangle shaped woad and such wonderful journalistic gems as . . .

Alle ye wolves whistell aftere Gudrun Middenheap. Thisse shapeley 17 years olde lasse loves travele ande meetinge people ande wantes to becume either a hussewife or a nonne. Nonne better Gudrun! What a waste!! Minde yew t'would be nice to get into ye habit God wot!!!

THE NAUSEMEN

After the Angled Saxons came the Vikings in their boats full of butter and bacon, teak coffee tables and fish-shaped glass ashtrays with dragon heads and Kirk Douglas on the front (of the boat of course, not the ashtrays). They frightened the crap out of the Northumbrians establishing Danelaw and Danegeld and the custom of riding bicycles without saddles.

Viking words that came into English from the Old Norse (cf. Old Norse's Almanac) are:

Ow!
Ouch!!
Ooh!!
Help!!
Don't forget the gas meter Olaf
and *Die you bugger die!!!.*

The Scandinavian invaders also introduced the apostrophe and produced an Early Norse Reader, The Ladybird Olaf and Helga books.

Anselm is a monk.
Anselm writes books.
'Here come the boats!!' says Anselm.
See Anselm.
See Anselm run.
Look! Anselm has no head.

After the Nausemen nothing much happened and people started repeating themselves.

THE NOTHING MUCH HAPPENED PERIOD

After the Nausemen nothing much happened and English stagnated for a while. People were quite miserable and expected to be raped or pillaged or both at any minute. The winters were long and crabs came frozen home in pails so that for a couple of hundred years language existed mainly of sighs and grunts and conversation was limited to discussions on wallpaper and haemorrhoids. This was called The Dark Ages.

CLAP HANDS HERE COMES NORMAN!!!

The French invaded in 1066, as every schoolperson knows, and introduced a lot of foppish, limp-wristed words into the language like *royal, count, meringue* and *coq au vin.*

They also rendered the number sixty-nine useless to all serious intents and purposes.

They did however help sort out some of the spelling problems that had been around for some time. In particular they introduced *q* and *u* into the language as a combination to replace the Old English combination *cw.*

Thus *cwealm* became *qualm* and *cweue* became *queue* and therefore meant that you could score a lot more at SCRABBLE than before.

This was really the only contribution the French made to the English language. Although it must not be forgotten that they also gave us lots of hard-to-pronounce words for pretty ordinary food so that waiters in yuppie restaurants could laugh at us and we could end up ordering the tune the band was playing instead of:

Pommes de Terre Frites – chips
Coquille St. Jacques – mashed potatoes and cod.

It was about this time also that the diphthong entered English. Now I don't know about you but I actually think that diphthongs

can be extremely dangerous in the wrong hands and it's probably also time that gerunds were outlawed. Gerunds and diphthongs are anathema to any God-fearing English speaker and it is a little-known fact that gerunds and diphthongs are the only parts of speech that you can catch by deep kissing or heavy petting.

THE ARRIVAL OF LOW DUTCH

After the French invasion and before Chaucer and Shakespeare nothing much of any real worth was written in English and nothing much happened except that some Low Dutchmen came from Holland on a hooker, smoking pipes and wearing clogs and going into a bar in Cheapside introduced a lot of new words into English. Thus when you say to a landlord selling keg beer: This **booze** is **crap,** you are speaking Low Dutch but also very good and almost certainly truthful English.

THE GREAT VOWEL SHIFT

It was also about this time that the Great Vowel Shift occurred. Nobody really knows what this was but it is said to have been drastic. People all over Europe couldn't understand each other for years because all their vowels had shifted overnight. There had been what is now called a Great Vowel Movement.

People walked around saying
'Hoo are yo?'
When they meant to ask
'How are you?' and
'Fork Arf yo pollick!'
when they meant that they wanted the person in question to go away.

THE INVENTION OF JOURNALISM

After The Great Vowel Shift, all was confusion until Caxton came along and invented printing and then everyone knew what a vowel looked like and at the next meeting of the English Parliament they agreed that they would only use five vowels and always in the same place. Thus ended the Irritable Vowel Syndrome, Loose Vowels and the Great Vowel Shift.

Caxton also invented the full stop, the blank space and the comma which was great since writers now had a means of preventing all the words from running together and falling off the page. He also invented the colon and the semi-colon which nobody has ever found a use for.

Unfortunately he also invented journalism for which no one will

ever forgive him since for every James Cameron there are eleven million little shits who shouldn't be allowed out with a Papermate and a piece of paper.

THE AGE OF SHAKESPEARE

After all this came the Age of Shakespeare which has produced so much good language.

Shakespeare at his word processor

Shakespeare was a genius and had the largest vocabulary of anybody in the whole history of the English language except for a boy in our school who could swear for an hour and forty minutes without repeating himself.

The Age of Shakespeare was followed by a man called Doctor Johnson who said *'Every man likes the smell of his own farts'* and then sat down and wrote a dictionary from which he omitted most of the swearwords current at the time because he wanted to keep them to himself.

Dr Johnson had a friend called Boswell who snooped on him and wrote down everything he said until Dr Johnson caught him doing this one night in a pub called The Ruptured Highwayman on the Great North Road and brained him with a cuspidor. Thus perish all plagiarists.

By the time of Dr Johnson, English had begun to settle down. It had a lot of loan words from the French, Dutch and Latin and a few old Norse and Celtic bits as well. It stayed this way largely until this century when there was a great influx of American words which came over here during World War II via American comic books, films and television.

To the Americans we owe

SHAZAM
SPLAT
KERPOW
VAROOM
KERANG
PLAY IT AGAIN SAM!
TO THE BAT-CAR ROBIN!!
WHAT'S UP DOC?
HAMBURGER
PRETZEL
MILKSHAKE
MUFFDIVING
JITTERBUG and
'NUKE 'EM BACK INTO THE STONE AGE!!!!'

...where we can all start again with *'See Ug. See Ug run. Ug has three legs. See Spot the dog. Spot has no legs. Spot has wings, a big beak and barks and wags his tail'*.

THE WAGES OF SIN. DO YOU
KNOW WHAT IS HAPPENING CHUMS?
(CLUE: THE YOUNG LADY IS NOT SELLING
POTATOES)

'THIS IS THE LAST TIME I GO SWIMMING AT
SELLAFIELD' SHRIEKED TRACEY

'AW COME ON LENIN! WE ONLY
NEED ONE MORE FOR AN UPRISING'

It is the year 2088. BBC Radio 63 is broadcasting the three hundred thousandth edition of Gardener's Question Time live from the village hall of Much Nookie in the Marsh, North Yorkshire.

The Greenhouse effect has resulted in the partial melting of both polar ice caps and a one hundred and sixty foot increase in the sea level world-wide, one result of which is that Britain is now a series of islands of varying size stretching from Dartmoor to Pitlochry. The majority of the population now live in the Scottish Highlands. The Pope is the head of the Meteorological Office and the Weather Forecast has been replaced by 'Prayers to God About the Climate.'

The average mean temperature is 88° Fahrenheit dropping to minus sixteen in the winter and rising to 104° F in the height of summer. People have only just got over chilblains when they are struck down by sunstroke.

CHAIRMAN

We are here today in the picturesque village of Much Nookie in the Marsh in Yorkshire at the invitation of the Much Nookie Camel Ranchers, Cactus Growers and Allotments Society. The soil around here is largely dust of an alkaline nature.

Our panel today consists of Professor Stefan Digalotsky of Mumps University, Fred Piles from the Ashton and Stalybridge

ENER'S N TIME

Archipelago, Bill Sowerbum of the Yeovil Island Fish Farm and Nora Radish, first lady captain of the Birmingham to Swindon Ferry.

Our first question comes from Mrs Ivy Clingon.

MRS CLINGON

I have repeatedly tried to grow edible tumbleweed to supplement my family's diet. But each year the kangaroos get over the fence and kick the tumbleweed out of the garden where the slugs eat it.

CHAIRMAN

Fred – kangaroos and tumbleweed – more in your patch this.

FRED

How big are the kangaroos?

MRS CLINGON

Between sixteen and twenty feet.

FRED

Well Mrs Clingon it sounds to me as though you've really crapped out here! At that size you can't exactly go and shoo them away. If one of those buggers jumped on you it'd be a wooden overcoat job! Have you thought of shooting them?

MRS CLINGON

My husband did try once but the kangaroos took his gun off him and beat his brains out with it.

CHAIRMAN
That's terrible! What did you do?

MRS CLINGON
Well we mixed him in with some John Innes Number Four Composting Mixture and some tea leaves and ash and dug him into the prickly pear patch.

CHAIRMAN
Stefan?

STEFAN

Well it sounds to me as though you've done exactly the right thing there Mrs Clingon. I think you might have considered adding three parts sharp sand and one part of lizard manure to the patch, because you know butchered husband does take a while to compost down.

But all the old style gardeners will tell you that slugs can be dealt with quite simply by erecting an electric fence forty feet from the house so that you have a chance to go and retrieve the tumbleweed after the kangaroos have gone and before the slugs get to it.

CHAIRMAN

Nora, you've got something to say about slugs I believe.

NORA

Are the slugs the species *Slimensis slipperensi*, six foot long with two heads and a mouthful of teeth like a mechanical digger?

MRS CLINGON

These are actually nearer ten foot long. We live quite close to Sellafield you see. We tried putting salt on them but the helicopter got pecked out of the sky by a young sparrow.

NORA
There is one thing that just might work. In my garden in Solihull we were troubled with slugs until my husband borrowed a laser cannon from the local riot police. We found that after three weeks intensive fighting our garden was quite free of them.

CHAIRMAN
Bill?

BILL
Well I think some of this new-fangled stuff can do more harm than good. My old father always used to tie a piece of meat to a tree as a decoy and hide big lumps of concrete in the branches. He got one of us kids to hide in the tree and when the slug went for the meat we dropped a lump of concrete on its head. Quite simple, ridiculously cheap and just as effective as any of your modern methods. And these old gardeners knew their stuff you know because of course the slug didn't vaporise so it went on the compost heap afterwards.

CHAIRMAN.
So there you are Mrs Clingon. Not much we can do about the kangaroos, but some good advice regarding the slugs.

Our next question please.

MR JANUS
Hugh Janus. My problem is gila monsters in the melon patch. I've tried everything including keeping a chained condor but the gila monsters still manage to destroy the crop most years.

CHAIRMAN
Well this sounds as though it might be more in Stefan's line. Stefan, gila monsters in the melon patch.

STEFAN
It's a funny thing with gila monsters. Some years there hardly seems to be any of them about and yet other years we're overrun with them. Their only natural enemy of course is the Giant Dormouse and when the Dormouse has a bad year the gila monster seems to flourish. This year of course the sandstorms have decimated the dormouse population so there you are. Up to your knees in gila monsters. Now what can you do?

Well I always recommend three parts fine loam to one part sharp sand for gila monsters. But try coating the melons with something that tastes nasty. Try rubbing a few old McDonalds' burgers on them. That should do the trick.

CHAIRMAN
Bill?

BILL
Well these new fangled ideas are all well and good but when I was a lad my old dad used to just send us kids out wearing metal boots to kick 'em to death; and do you know it's still as good a method as . . .
At this point the broadcast was terminated when a forty ton pigeon landed on the roof of the building causing the immediate deaths of everyone in it.

THE END

Copyright BBC Enterprises, Broadcasting House, Isle of Chipping Sodbury.

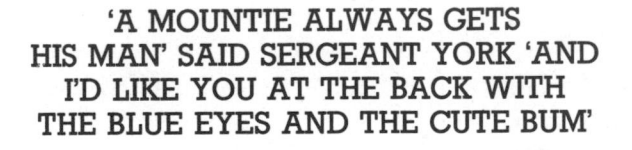

'A MOUNTIE ALWAYS GETS
HIS MAN' SAID SERGEANT YORK 'AND
I'D LIKE YOU AT THE BACK WITH
THE BLUE EYES AND THE CUTE BUM'

'YOU'VE MADE A BUGGER OF IT
THIS TIME FAIRY GODMOTHER!' NEIGHED
CINDERELLA PEEVISHLY.

A VERY SHORT
IN FACT INCREDIBLY SHORT
HISTORY OF THE WORLD
PART ONE

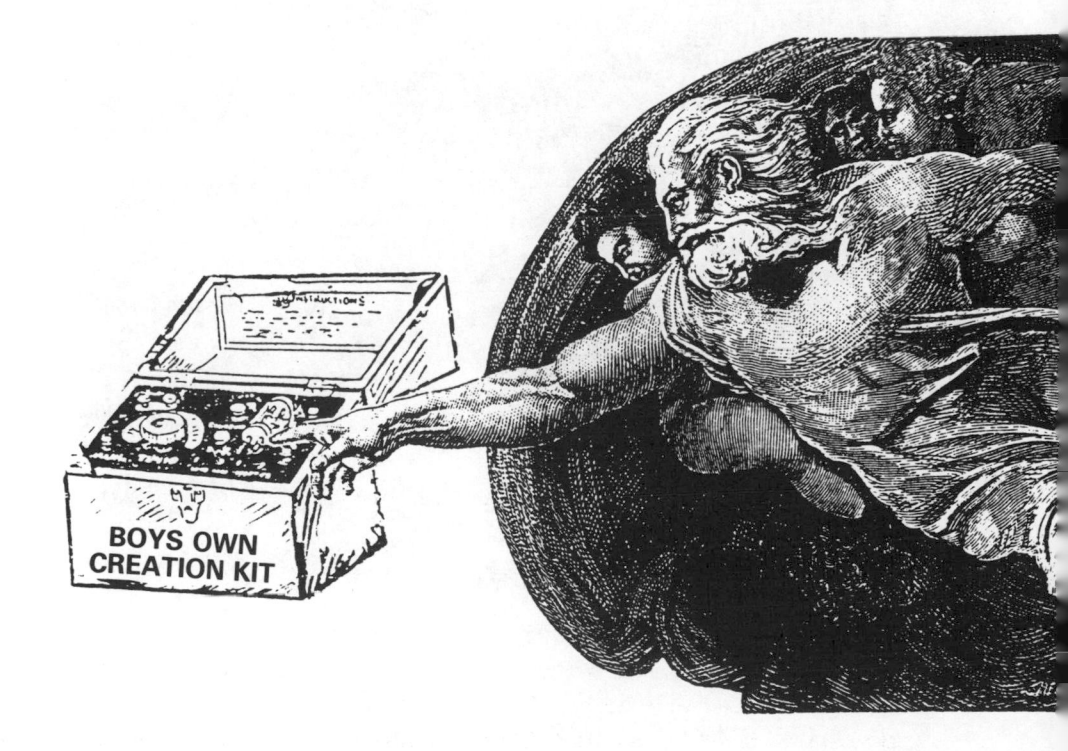

BOYS OWN
CREATION KIT

The entry for Big G's diary year dot, week one, Monday morning reads:

Woke up this morning feeling lousy. Too much Ambrosia last night. Holy Ghost and J C feeling lousy too. Three hangovers in one gives a new meaning to the concept of The Trinity. Pretty hard to handle for someone who 'Is, always has been and always will be'. The eternal hangover, dreadful prospect.

Opened Christmas present to self and found Boy's Own Creation Kit.

Instructions simple.

Batteries not included. Do not throw away plastic bag or put over head. Add water and press button.

Pressed button.

Big Bang!

Funny little planet appears.

Went back to bed.

Troubled.

Three in bed.

Holy Ghost hogging covers.

JC falls on floor.

It seems therefore that the Big Bang Theory of the creation is true, in part at least. Modern physicists have yet to come up with the 'Add Water and Press Button' hypothesis.

So there was a Big Bang.

A funny little planet emerged.

At first it was full of poisonous gases.

Nothing could live there.

Then Life appeared.

The first forms of Life were just microbes and squidgy little things that are now found only in your socks or the waist bands of certain undergarments.

There was a lot of radiation about at that time left over from the Big Bang.

The microbes and squidgy things ate the radiation when it had gone past the 'sell by' date.

This made them mutate.

There were all sorts of terrible mutations – some too fearful to behold.

Bug eyed monster loonies living in the Home Counties and writing letters to *The Times* about immigrants.

Fifty foot high balls of aggressive navel fluff.

Crop-haired, Doc Martens-wearing, lager-drinking young men with the IQs of garden snails who worked on the floor of the Stock Exchange, owned Filofaxes, drank Perrier water and drove Porsche cars.

Things that went trump in the night.

Time share salesmen.

Town planners.

Tory politicians.

Fortunately most of these mutations died out.

But one dismal day another, stranger mutation appeared.

It happened like this. Mrs. Big G. was defrosting and cleaning the freezer out one morning when She came upon something at the bottom; something long neglected; something furry, squidgy and horrible with no label on it, just lying there, lurking in a Sainsbury's bag. The 'sell by' date when She checked it was about three millennia gone and strange smells and noises were coming from the bag.

She was so horrified by the way this thing looked and smelt that she gave a terrible shriek and threw it out of the window.

through the infinities of deep space it fell, past Burton's Top Shop and the Drive-in Planetary McDonalds' landing with a bump on that funny little new planet smack in the centre of Eden New Town.

The wrapping fell off, most of the mouldy bits fell off and out stepped two poor bare, forked little animals with no fur and even less sense.

These were of course Mr and Mrs Cro-Magnon.

Next morning the two man-type things went wandering round Creation hand in hand, all pink and wrinkly (as against Alcock and Brown).

The two Pink and Wrinkly things moved through the park.

Eden Municipal Gardens said a sign. **Opening Hours dawn till dusk. No ball games. No cycling. No forbidden fruit eating. By Order.**

Near the bandstand was a bronze statue of a big figure looking stern and important.

Underneath was the legend

Alderman Big G

Lord Mayor of Creation.

A passing snake handed them an aerosol

'Looks a funny old thing to me,' said one of the Pink and Wrinkly things – the one who was definitely not Alcock and Brown.

'S'dead borin 'ere,' said the other Pink and Wrinkly thing with bumps on its chest.

A passing snake handed them an aerosol.

'Go on,' it said, 'You'll like it!'

'BIG G SUCKS !!', wrote the Pink and Wrinkly things on the statue. Off they walked.

'Let's get a pint of lager and break somefink!' said one of them.

'Good idea!' said the other.

Into the Jolly Mutant they strolled.

'Uh oh!! here comes trouble,' said the Orc.

'They look alright to me,' said the Dodo.

'Give 'em time,' said the Whale.

'If you ask me, it's time Big G. invented some social workers,' said the landlord wiping a beer glass with his apron.

After that a lot of time passed.

Then Big G. found the graffiti on the statue.

As you may read in Genitals Chap IV Verses 21-26 . . .

And it did come to pass that the Lord one morning at walk in the fields of Him didst find his image and likeness and it was defaced and he did go potty crying.

'Yeah though thou comest to me in thy nakedness wherefore art thou now clothed in fig leaves?' And unto him did cry the Pink and Wrinkly thing.

'Have you tried walkin' through these bleedin' 'olly bushes with yer weddin' tackle unboxed? It's piggin' painful pal I can tell you!'

'Less of thy lip,' saith the Lord.

'Bog off!!' said the Pink and Wrinkly thing.

'Don't let him talk to you like that Wayne. He's a bleedin' head-the-ball,' cried his helpmeet. 'Smack him on the nose.'

And it came to pass that Wayne did stick the nut on Big G.

'Right!' said Big G. holding his noseth. 'I've got me mad up now!!' And it came to pass that the Lord did call upon a park keeper to drive them thence with a torch and a length of barbed wire.

'We'll be back!' shouted the Pink and Wrinklies.

'Yeah and I say unto thee don't be so sure,' said Alderman Big G. shutting the gates firmly behind them.

Then as the Bible tells us there was a lot of begetting in the Abomination of Desolation New Town Apartments. Ahab begat Mohab who begat Ehab who begat Ohab, Uhab and Prefab. In fact as the Bible says, *Yeah it did come to pass and they were at it like knives. There was all manner of bonking and yeah even*

the hedgehog was not safe.

The Pink and Wrinklies begat lots more Pink and Wrinklies. Then when they ran out of names ending in 'ab', they invented lots more names so that they would know who had begat what and when, so that the Inland Revenue would know where to send the forms to.

MAN THE TOOL USER

It was about this time that Man discovered tools. They were in an old chest of drawers at the back of the garage behind the sledge and the inflatable paddling pool with the hole in it.

51

It was a good job he did so too because people were fed up of knocking nails in with their heads and felling trees with their teeth. It is this use of tools that distinguishes Man from other animals. Can you imagine what would have happened if sheep had got to the tools first? We would have been walking round eating grass and the sheep would have been wearing Kiddieswool sweaters from Jaeger and eating Manchops with mint sauce.

Having all these tools around meant that Man had more time for rumpo and wasn't as dizzy and sick on account of not having to knock nails in with his head or plough with his feet. This resulted in a population explosion.

THE COMING OF CIVILISATION

When there were enough of the little Pink and Wrinkly things they invented civilisation.

The first civilisation was Ur of the Chaldees where they cut down all the trees around the headwaters of the rivers. There were flash floods for years which destroyed most of Ur and made a desert out of it.

'We didn't know what we were doing!' said the Pink and Wrinkly things.

Then came the Greeks and Romans.

The Greeks invented Philosophy and Doner Kebabs. Philosophy is the art of mental gymnastics which when perfected allows one to vanish up one's own rectum.

Greek civilisation collapsed out of boredom and a surfeit of Doner Kebabs and Philosophy and also because the Greeks cut down all the trees and the soil washed away and there was not enough food for everyone.

'We didn't know what we were doing!' said the little Greek Pink and Wrinkly things and promptly invited SunMed over to turn them into a theme park.

Roman civilisation collapsed because the sewers backed up causing plague and disease and because they too had cut down all the trees and the soil had washed away and there was not enough food for everyone.

'We didn't know what we were doing!' said the Romans hurriedly inventing ice cream, spaghetti, dark glasses and the famous Italian sport of walking on the water wearing concrete wellingtons.

After that there was the Dark Ages during which Europe was ravaged by hordes of Goths, Visigoths, Vandals and Manchester United supporters.

Following the Dark Ages there was the Renaissance. There were no World Empires at that time, just small city states and kingdoms.

Then along came the Multi-Nationals.

As a result of the growth of navies, the establishment of armies and the rise of a successful merchant class the first Multi-Nationals started to look around for market opportunities, take-over possibilities and outlet expansion.

The Portuguese and Spanish Multi-Nationals promptly set off and raped, pillaged and hacked their way through South America all in the name of Big G. destroying civilisations older and finer than any in Europe.

'They sacrifice people in the name of the Big G. of the Sun,' cried the Spaniards, putting thousands of Indians to death in the name of Big G., the Jesuits and Trade.

'Nothing but savages!' said the Portuguese shooting them for fun on a Sunday after church.

But fear not for *HERE COME THE ENGLISH.*

'Cor stripe me pink! Lumme!' said Good Queen Bess. 'The Spaniards are doin' all the business wiv the gold an' that. 'Ere Raleigh go and feeve it orf 'em!'

And in an operation that makes the Brinks-Mat robbery look puerile, Good Queen Bess (riddled with hereditary syphilis according to some historians), dispatched her trusty Sea Dogs to patrol the sea lanes and knock off anything they could. And they did.

The Spaniards, rightly pigged off with this, sent an Armada to England. Storms destroyed most of the Armada and the English fleet the rest.

'We wuz robbed!!' said the Spaniards. How right they were.

The Spanish Empire then collapsed because its agriculture was falling about as a result of deforestation, overgrazing etc. and because the House of Hapsburg, through interbreeding, had developed lower jaws so stuck out that they couldn't chew their food.

A SHORT NOTE ON THE THEORY OF THE DIVINE RIGHT OF KINGS

The theory of the Divine Right of Kings was a theory (largely devised by the kings themselves) that a King is Big G.'s representative on Earth and anybody who didn't agree with that didn't agree with Big G. and was therefore a heretic – the punishment for heresy being death. Pretty neat, eh?

Now let's look at some of the examples of Big G.'s Representatives on Earth.

King Henry VIII, probably syphilitic, certainly a hypocrite, almost definitely unhinged. Wrote a treatise in defence of the Papacy earning himself the accolade Def Fid (which until recently appeared on all British coinage). Then finding that the Pope would not grant him a divorce from his dead brother's widow, proclaimed himself head of the Church in England, cut off the head of his best friend Sir Thomas More and dissolved the monasteries to make plenty of loot since he himself was well short of scratch having been wrestling with a Frenchman called the Dolphin, in a field made entirely out of gold cloth.

His daughter Good Queen Bess, lauded by Tory historians as a sort of cross between Marilyn Monroe and Julius Caesar, was in fact a raddled hag, more a cross between Jack the Ripper and Minnie Mouse, who hounded Catholics throughout the land, burning and disembowelling them and continued her father's policy of the destruction of the monastic houses.

Her reign extended of course to Ireland where she carried on a regime of oppression and persecution that has carried on to this day turning the Irish into 'the Blacks of Europe'. She also wore sexy black underwear made from the woven nasal hair of dead monks, but only when there was an X in the month.

King Carlos The Mad of Spain, one of the last of the Hapsburg House, had a jaw so underslung other people had to chew his food for him and he once hiccuped and bit his nose off. The

A cross between Marilyn Monroe and Julius Caesar

historian A.J.P.Taylor says in his book *European History Wednesday the 13th to Friday the 15th February 1603, It is the considered opinion of most historians from Carlyle to Tate and Lyle that this chap was without any doubt a total barmpot.* Refusing to accept that his wife was dead he kept her corpse beside him in bed for months until the corpse eventually mummified.

King George III of England was well round the twist and was convinced for part of his life that he was a frog and used to hop around the floor in front of visitors.

Queen Victoria presided over the birth of the British Empire which resulted in the enslavement of millions of people and prepared the way for the first of a series of world wars that has gone on ever since. The First World War was in fact a war between countries whose rulers were cousins and was fought, not to save 'poor little Belgium', but because the Germans were mad at Queen Victoria for buying the same curtains as the Kaiser. Relations deteriorated from that point and reached war pitch when the little Kaiser's ball went into King Edward's garden and broke a cucumber frame.

'Shit! That's it!' shouted the King. 'Where's me diary? Right, let's 'ave a butcher's ook. I've nothing on for the next four years. We'll 'ave a war.'

It was, by the way, a little foot soldier in the Germany Army of the First World War, one Private Shicklegrubber who later went on to change his name to Adolf Hitler. Ring a bell?

It was Queen Victoria who, when asked by her daughter what she should do on her wedding night, said, 'Lie back and think of England', which she did.

But when she thought of Morecambe she burst out laughing and spoiled everything.

It would be ungentlemanly here and probably beyond the bounds of Historical Scholarship to even mention the rumour that John Brown, the Queen's favourite gillie, was giving her one.

Very old Queen Victoria joke that did not appear in Punch, *told to me by Spike Milligan:*

Queen Victoria 'Is anything worn under your kilt John?'

John Brown 'Och!! No ma'am!! It's in as guid a werrkin order as it iver was. Jings! Cribbens! Help ma boab!'

LOUIS XIV

A very interesting frog king who had two stomachs and who built

a palace called Versailles on a swamp causing the deaths of thousands of workers. Unfortunately the architect forgot to include any toilets so that people used to go behind curtains, in drawers, flower vases and anywhere else they could find. (A Louis XIV George III was auctioned at Sotheby's recently for 2 million pounds.)

It was Louis who ultimately so degraded the French Aristocracy and so destroyed the French Economy that his son found himself inheriting the French Revolution. This led to the Rain of Terror which just goes to show that the weather was every bit as bad in those days as it is now. During those days of terror a man called Dr Guillotine invented a game called 'Head the Basket'. It was very popular and was a sort a precursor to listening to the radio as an accompaniment to knitting.

'Is anything worn under your kilt John?

57

Not long after the French Revolution came along a man called Napoleon who proclaimed himself Emperor (another word for King). He was a fingernail junkie with an incurable and expensive habit. He chewed his nails so badly that he kept his hand inside his vest so that nobody would see the ragged ends of his fingers.

Other politicians like Wellington used to invite him round to tea so that they could laugh at his stumps. All this gave him so many headaches that he kept saying, 'Not tonight Josephine.'

Napoleon went to war against almost everybody so that his name was used to frighten English children to bed.

'Go to sleep or Boney will come and tear your eyes out, bite your bum and disembowel you,' crooned loving mothers to their infants as they rocked them in the cradle.

That was about the time that Lord Nelson fought the French fleet and got wounded in the cockpit.

'Kiss it Hardy,' he said. And we all know what the answer was to that.

Napoleon, by the way, is rumoured to have had a very small willy as against a large Scotch.

Silly Napoleon joke.

What are you drinking Boney – a large Martini?

No, I'll have a small willy and a dash of lemonade, please.

Here endeth the short discourse on the Divine Right of Kings.

To recap.

History can be divided into Ages (we historians like to do this since it makes things a bit neater and gives us things to write about).

So first of all we had the

PREHISTORIC AGE (Pink and Wrinkly to Chaldean)

this was followed by the age of the

EARLY CIVILISATIONS (Romans to Dark Ages)

then came

THE AGE OF EMPIRE (Renaissance to Victoria)

and we now come to the last age of all

THE INDUSTRIAL AGE.

A VERY QUICK NOTE ON THE GOLDEN AGE AND THEN WE'LL GET ON

Some historians claim that there was a Golden Age when Good

58

Tories ruled the land and everybody lived in pretty little cottages that are now fetching £200,000 (have you any idea how much it's worth now?) danced round Maypoles and sang 'hey nonny no' and touched their forelocks to the squire who looked after them all and gave them parties at Christmas and they all died and got buried under the elms in the country churchyard.

This is one hundred per cent bull.

There was a Golden Age.

It lasted for about three weeks a long time ago and ended when one of the Golden Agers said 'I've got an idea. We have to have leaders because some people are cut out to be leaders and leaders should be better rewarded than everybody else because . . . erm because erm. . . . . anyway I now declare myself King!!!'

'Just a minute,' said one of the Golden Agers putting up his hand.

'Cut his head off!!' said the King.

'Please Sire may we lick your botty?' said all the other people.

THE INDUSTRIAL AGE

There had always been industry about. Metal had been mined, coal had been dug, cloth had been woven from the Earliest Times.

Then came the discovery that it made your hands dirty.

'Wayne, you got in bed with your boots on last night and now there's coal dust all over me nightie!'

'Sorry Sharon. It's the coal. It's very black you know.'

'Well, it's not good enough. What's the milkman going to say if he sees me like this? You'll have to get some poor people to dig the coal up for you, that's all.'

And so he did.

Meanwhile there was trouble at t'mill.

The discovery that some of the looms were very small and hard to clean resulted in the employment of circus midgets as under-loom cleaners and the cancellation of Snow White and the Seven Dwarfs at the Rochdale Empire.

A further discovery that children of four were not human beings resulted in the employment and deaths of large numbers of them in the mills and mines of Merrie Olde Englande.

Many four year olds, to escape the mills and mines, lied about their age by smoking and drinking and claiming to be twenty-one.

'Right!' said the factory owners, 'twenty-one years old and two foot six!! – you must be midgets then. Get down the pit.'

'Don't we have any alternative?' asked the children.

'Yes,' said the factory owners, 'you can starve if you like.'

A man called Engels saw a lot of this going on and invited a man called Marx to Manchester where he sat in Chetham's library and wrote a lot of bits that later became *Das Kapital*, a sort of Scouting for Boys guide to Communism.

In Russia a form of king called the Tsar had so mismanaged the country that there had been great hardship and massive famine resulting in the deaths by dying of millions of people.

Communism brought about the Russian Revolution which resulted in the massacre of millions of innocent people and great hardship and famine.

Then along came a man called Joe Stalin who continued the old Communist traditions of famine and the massacre of millions of innocent people.

The Second World War (which was really World War One Part Two) resulted in the deaths of millions of innocent people.

Towards the end of the War at a place called Yalta, the Whole World was divided up by three old men called Stalin, Roosevelt and Churchill, into 'spheres of influence'.

This was to result in the Cold War which was not cold at all but very hot and has resulted in the deaths of millions of innocent people in Cambodia, Vietnam, Burma, Aden, Palestine, the Persian Gulf, Chile, Nicaragua, Korea and El Salvador.

As well as producing Wars, the Age of Industry was also very good at producing pollution.

This was first noticed when a coughing albatross fell out of the sky and landed on some Londoners killing them.

'It's nothing to do with the factories,' said the factory owners.

'It's just a bad year for albatrosses.'

Then a lot of fish died.

'They probably drowned,' said the industrialists. 'Breathing all that water gave them damp on the chest.'

Then a lot of children near atom plants got leukaemia.

'They were just unlucky,' said the scientists, 'and anyway you can't prove anything. They probably got it sitting on cold doorsteps. The nuclear industry is the safest industry there is.'

Then somebody in a place called Chernobyl said, 'I wonder what this button does?'

'Ooops!' said the scientists, hurriedly explaining that it couldn't happen outside Russia.

Then sheep and lambs produced higher than normal readings of Caesium.

Silly lamb joke specially for my daughter, Emma, who likes sheep

First lamb	*What are you reading?*
Second lamb	*Caesium.*
First lamb	*Is it about the Roman bloke?*
Second lamb	*No.*
First lamb	*Any good?*
Second lamb	*Once you've started it you can't put it down.*

'Chernobyl,' said the scientists.

But the sheep were all near Sellafield and Trawsfynydd nuclear plants.

'A fluke,' said the scientists.

'Bollix!!' said the farmers, many of whom had wondered why their sheep glowed in the dark.

Then a lot of trees died because of acid rain.

'It's aliens from outer space,' said the industrialists.

'We can't stop it now anyway because there's too much involved,' said some of the industrialists.

'I don't give a monkeys,' said some others cutting down the rain forest.

And some gases went into the air and destroyed the ozone layer and other gases kept in the sun's heat, melting the ice caps. And the forests died and the soil washed away and that was the end of THE INDUSTRIAL AGE.

'What's the next age?' asked one of the little Pink and Wrinkly things.

'It says 'ere in the paper that it's cancelled,' said another.

'The Cancelled Age – that's a funny name for it. Let's 'ave a look at that paper. 'Ere look at the Bristols on that! I wouldn't mind givin' 'er a seein' to. 'Ere pass us that can of lager will yer.'

So then came

THE CANCELLED AGE.

'We didn't know what we were doing!' said the little Pink and Wrinkly things.

And after that ...

There was a funny little planet.

And it was full of poisonous gases.

And nothing could live there.

'Just a minute. Let's have another look at them instructions,' said Big G.

THE END

SAFE SEX FOR BOYS

SOLO POSITIONS

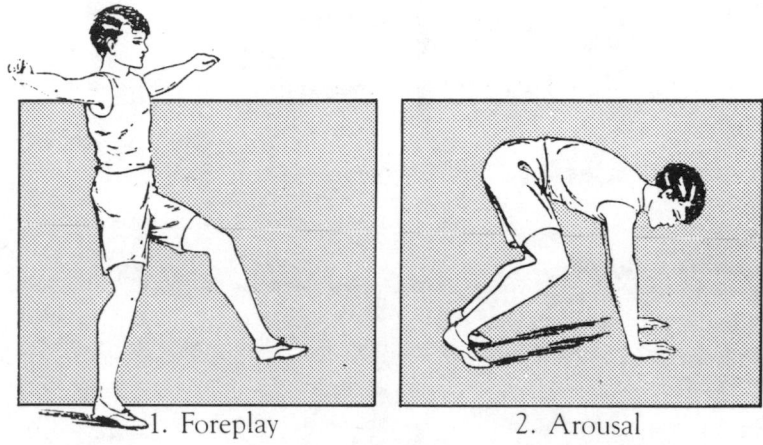

1. Foreplay   2. Arousal

3. Climax   4. Learning to walk again

SAFE SEX

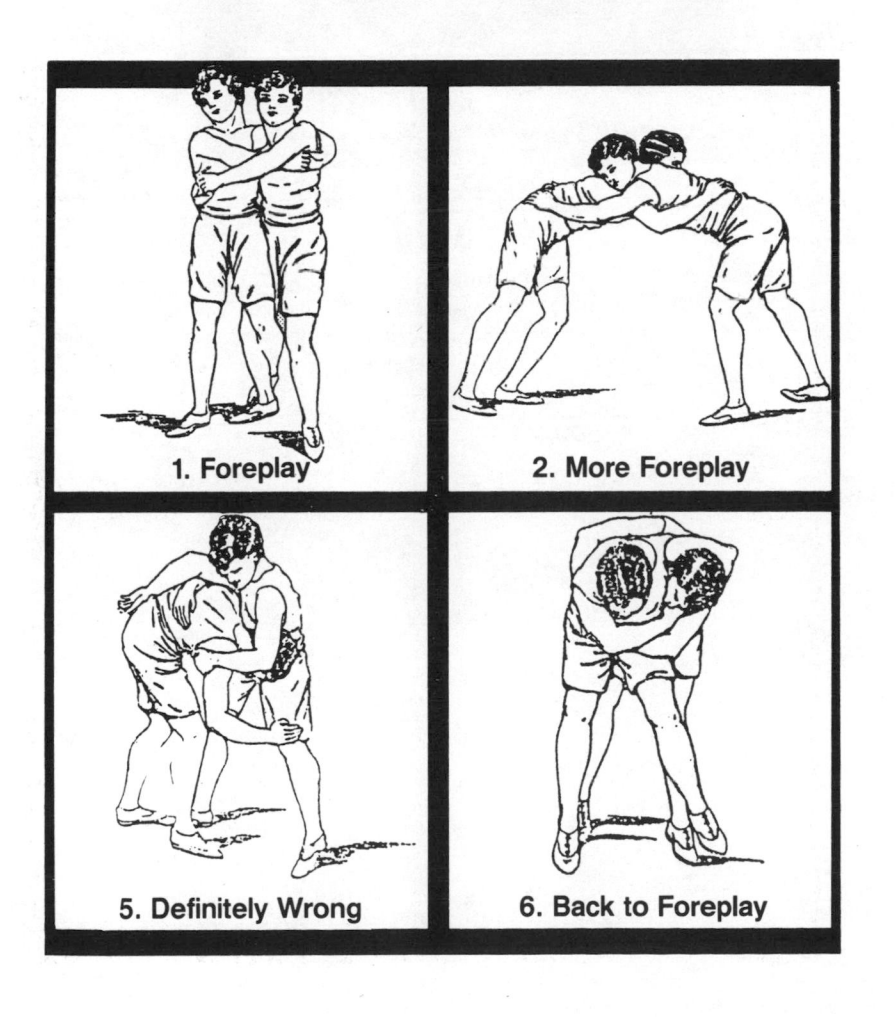

1. Foreplay

2. More Foreplay

5. Definitely Wrong

6. Back to Foreplay

FOR BOYS
DOUBLES

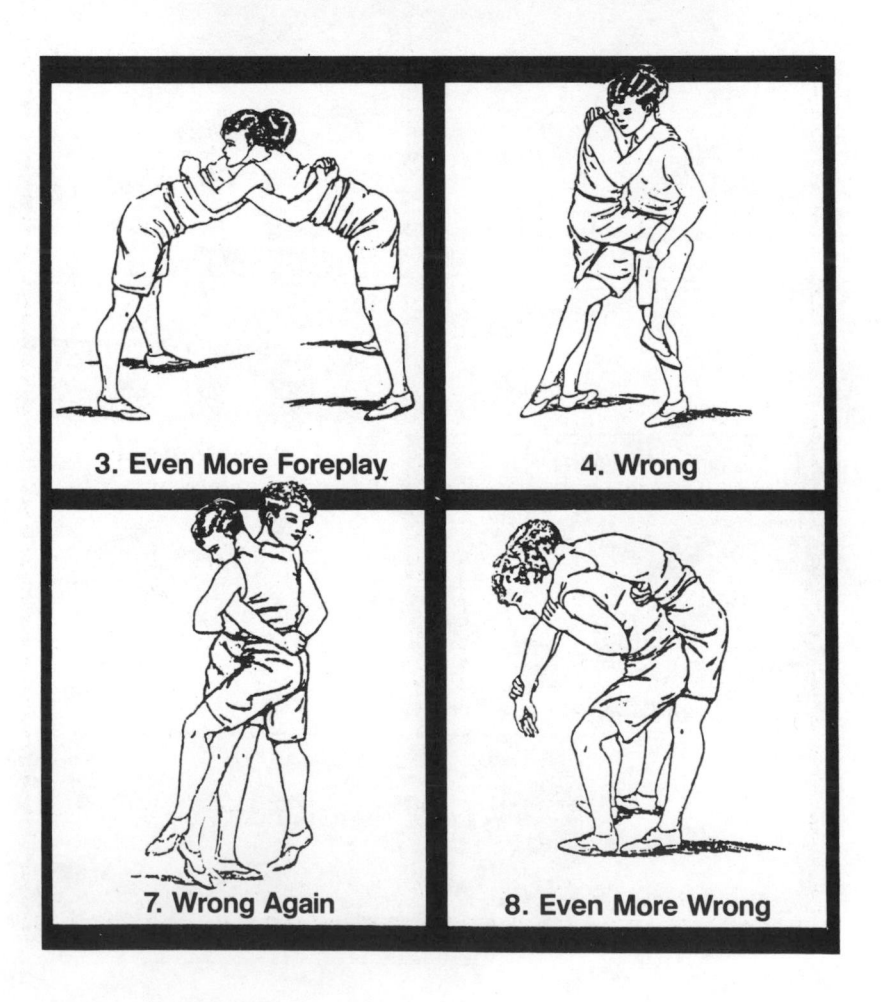

3. Even More Foreplay

4. Wrong

7. Wrong Again

8. Even More Wrong

SAFE SOLO SEX FOR BIGGER BOYS

1. FOREPLAY

2. FIVEPLAY

3. AROUSAL

4. FINAL POSITION

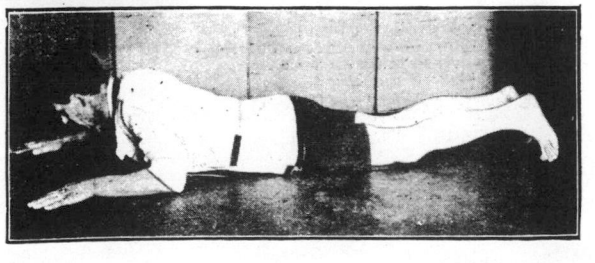

ADVANCE FARTING

1. THE "CLEARING
THE TABLE" POSITION

2. The "BLOWING THE DEAD
FLIES OFF THE CEILING
LAMP" POSITION

3. THE "KNOCKING THE
CAT INTO THE COAL
SCUTTLE" POSITION

Before Jones could stop him Maltravers had sabotaged the Peewit patrols condom.

"Mother!" cried Emily, "you cancelled the papers and milk but you forgot to cancel the babies! We could have been burgled!"

SPONSORED BY NEIGHBOURHOOD WATCH

ONE OF THE WORLD'S MASTERPIECES IN BRONZE

RODIN'S "THE CONDOM MAKERS".

GREAT MOMENTS IN HISTORY 1

Fearful that television might dull his children's minds, Baron Rothschild bought them a pauper to watch

GREAT MOMENTS IN HISTORY

It was after that that Mr. Connolly decided to give up his job as Paul Daniels' assistant and try his hand as a comedian.

"Si Señor" roared Gomez. "Eet was Pancho and me putta da chilli powder in da condom".

DON'T LET THIS HAPPEN TO YOU!

"It's the results of my pregnancy test. I'm afraid you're going to be a father, Jennings Minor."

Red Spot condoms. Only £3.50 for two

RED SPOT  call FREEPHONE and ask for the "dial a condom" direct mail service.

"Admit it Bentley. It was you who let the hedgehogs loose in the condom factory

A MILLION FLIES
can't be wrong

To prove that anybody will drink Grottleys Bitter we took it half way up Everest and gave it the Sherpas to taste.

Their verdict – Crap!!

What can you expect when they've lived on a diet of rancid yak butter and British Mountaineering Council regulation biscuits all their lives.

GB Grottleys Bitter. The unreal ale.
All fizz and chemicals.
Served in kegs for Real Wallys.

An amazing NEW offer

THE
MEOWOPHONE

Amaze and delight your friends. Be the success of the party.
Everytime you press a key a hammer hits a tail! Remarkable innovation will interface with all BBC, Apple and Sinclair computers. Arrives fully tuned and house trained.
Runs all night on a saucer of milk.
Cat Litter extra.
No skill needed. Full instructional handbook supplied FREE. Send today to take advantage of our special launch offer price.

A DO IT YOURSELF SURGERY KIT

AN UNBEATABLE OFFER!

With absolutely no training you can perform appendectomies, vasectomies and many more operations including open heart surgery. All in the comfort of your own home.

Comes complete with our own home surgeons manual **"Snipping, Cutting and Tucking for Fun and Profit!"**

ONLY £259·99
COMPLETE

WRITE OR PHONE

The Rinkle Goolie restaurant invites you to savour our distinctive Asian cuisine.

Drunks specially catered for.
Fall asleep with your head on our pilaus!
Throw up on our forecourt.

Abuse our staff.
Open 8am – 2am.
Eight days a week.

THE RINKLE GOOLIE, POONA AVENUE
"To service you is our delight"

Pickit

NASAL HAIR DEPILATOR

Is an over abundance of nasal hair an embarrassment to you?
Does it trail in your soup?
Does it collect big greenies?
Dr. Stowricks amazing steam depilator removes excess nasal hair painfully, but successfully, clearing noses and tear ducts simultaneously.

Send today for completely free trial in the privacy of own nose.
Only £1.95 money back guarantee.

ANDREW LLOYD WEBBER &
ANDREW LLOYD WEBBER PRESENT:

WITCHY Poo!

The smash hit musical based on the real life story of The Lancashire Witches. Guaranteed to run for years! Only one rememberable song but a million pounds spent on production!!
It will dazzle! It will razzle! Real life burning at the stake!

"Amazing"	Sunday Telegraph
"Amazing"	Express
"Incredible"	Christian Science Monitor

"A bubbling cauldron of betwitching ballads"
P. O'Neil, Daily Mail

"Capitalist – middle class brainwashing justification of the sexist pogroms of 18th Century England"
Morning Star

At The Cambridge Circus for the next 10 years.
BOOK NOW FOR YOUR RETIREMENT OUTING.
SPECIAL RATES FOR OAP's.

COOKING One's CORGI

Pet dishes of H. M. the Queen

CORGI FOOL

This was always a great favourite with One's Children especially on hot afternoons at Balmoral. On those wonderful days when the thick swirling mist was warmer than normal, then One knew that summer had at last arrived in the Highlands.

This dish is wonderful served with Gillie's Fries and was one of my great great grandmother Victoria's favourites.

Serves four to six.

INGREDIENTS
1 medium sized corgi
Orange peel
Cream
Icing sugar

First fool the corgi by holding a stick in One's hand and making a throwing movement. Do not release the stick.

The corgi will run down One's lawn looking puzzledly for the stick.

Repeat this until the corgi is well fooled. Do not fool it too much or the corgi will lose heart and become flat and lifeless. When the corgi is well fooled, lift it onto the table and pretend to throw the stick into the blender. The corgi will then jump in.

Add the other ingredients and blend completely until the fool is a smooth mush.

One finds that if One places it in One's refrigerator then Corgi Fool becomes a dish fit for One. Serve with a dusting of chocolate powder and those rolled up biscuity things that One cannot remember the name of at present. Short of that One can always stick a Spratt's Oval in the middle. The charcoal ones are delish!

CORGI ROGAN JOSH

On One's trips around One's Commonwealth, One has come into contact with many tinted people and One finds that if they are treated like children then they are really quite acceptable. One has learnt this recipe from Mrs. Gandhi who of course is dead now but was not when she gave One this recipe. Mrs. Gandhi always reminded One of a tinted version of the dreadful tradesperson now in residence at No. 10.

One cooks this dish often for One's spouse who enjoys what he calls 'a good ring-stinger'. Known to One's children as Gandhi's Revenge, this dish is delicious served with Lassi.

INGREDIENTS

1 medium sized corgi (freshly plucked if possible)
2 onions
4 oz. red chillis
1 lb. fresh chillis
1 lb. garlic finely chopped
4 oz. freshly chopped root ginger
4 oz. mustard seed
1 tube Sloan's Liniment
2 oz. fresh coriander finely chopped
2 oz. fenugreek
1 oz. dhanhia
1 oz. cumin seed
1 lb. tomatoes
Ghee to fry

Fry the onions in the ghee until they are a golden brown. Then add all the spices, chillis and garlic.

By this time the corgi, having smelt the onions, will be off down the garden and hiding under a scottie's kilt. One has a lot of fun at Balmoral retrieving corgis from under scotties' kilts!

Once back in the kitchen firmly mallet one's corgi, sling it in the pan and cook until tender. Add the tomatoes and cook lightly until they go that funny squishy texture and the skins peel off.

Sprinkle with chopped coriander just before serving. Serve with boiled Patna rice, popadums and pickles.

One believes that in the North of England it is customary to drink a dozen pints of lager before eating this dish.

One finds this dish a great favourite with One's guests. But don't forget to place the toilet rolls in the refrigerator!

CORGI PUPS IN CUSTARD

A wonderful dish for children's parties, particularly since it is so bright and colourful and decorative. One has always found this to be a great success.

INGREDIENTS

1 puppy per child
1 gallon of milk
1 lb. custard powder.

Make the custard in the usual way. Pour into large bowl and when cooled to bloodwarm add the puppies. The puppies will swim around churning the custard up until it sets.

It is as well to be close at hand while this is happening in case one of the puppies tries to climb out. If this happens One mallets it lightly until it gets back in.

When the custard sets, One throws open the nursery doors and cries 'Children! Surprise! Surprise!'

WHOLE ROAST CORGI WITH HONEY AND LEMON SAUCE

Yet another dish fit for One! This dish is ideal for parties of ten or more. The preparation time is rather long but the fiddling is well worth One's effort One finds. The corgi (or corgis if it is an especially big affair) can be roasted either in the oven or on a spit.

Spitting One's corgi is a little awkward and can take a little practice before One becomes perfect, since they do tend to bite One!!

INGREDIENTS

1 extremely large and fat corgi
1 lb. honey
3 lemons
6 cloves

First pluck One's corgi. This is best done while the corgi is asleep. Then either spit or truss the corgi.

Stick the cloves evenly about the corgi then place in large bowl and pour over the marinade of lemon and honey. Leave overnight.

If One is cooking over an open fire instruct One's gardeners and footmen to prepare the fire while One makes ready the basting. If One is cooking in an oven turn knob to 375 degrees.

Roast corgi slowly, basting regularly. Serve on bed of rice or with usual vegetables. The collected sauce makes a wonderful gravy. Ensure that the corgi does not eat lemon and honey while in the bowl since this can taint the meat.

THICK CORGI AND PEA SOUP

A wonderful warming soup for those cold, misty, chilly-willy Balmoral days and so easy to make. Wonderful before an open fire with hot crusty bread.

INGREDIENTS

1 corgi
1 onion
1 lb. of dried peas (The sort that One's Northern Subjects call 'Blanket Lifters')
1 pint stock or One cube Knorr Corgi Stock.

For thick Corgi and Pea Soup One always uses the thickest corgi One can find. One first of all throws One's corgi a ball. If One's corgi looks puzzled then runs and bites a stone, One has usually found a thick corgi.

Fry the onion in the bottom of a large casserole until golden brown. Add corgi and peas. Boil until soup is good and thick stirring occasionally to prevent corgi from sticking to bottom. Yummy! Yummy!

Be careful not to eat this dish within twenty four hours of imbibing large quantities of Guinness. One finds that One coughs in One's trousers a great deal if One mixes mushy peas and Guinness!

QUICK CORGI CASSEROLE

Almost at the other end of the culinary spectrum from Thick Corgi and Pea Soup this recipe cries out for a particularly bright corgi, the sort that fetches One's slippers and nips the occasional Beefeater.

INGREDIENTS

1 quick Corgi
2 large onions
½ lb. carrots
½ lb. mushrooms
½ lb. potatoes
½ lb. tomatoes
1 pint red wine

Chop the onions coarsely. (To chop onions coarsely One shouts 'Stupid damn onions!' and 'Silly Bally Onions!' at them.) Fry until golden brown. Add vegetables and corgi and cover all with enough water to cook for three hours. When ready add wine and cook a little longer. Alternatively, drink wine and bugger One's guests if One gets a little tiddly is what One says! A short life and a merry one, what!

CORGI WELLINGTON

Of all dishes, One's favourite.

INGREDIENTS

I corgi
I fresh, green wellington
Mixed herbs and spices and salt to taste.

Insert corgi in wellington and cook until both are tender.

NEXT WEEK!!!!!!

Corgiburgers!
Corgipizza!
Jugged Corgi!
and many more mouth watering recipes!
All in your wonderful Daily Bumlicker!!!!

'WE SHOULD NEVER HAVE GIVEN PUSSKINS THAT
FISH FROM SELLAFIELD' HISSED GODFREY,
REACHING FOR THE SHOTGUN.

NURSE HARVEY'S PATENT EAR WAX
REMOVER IN OPERATION.
REMOVES EAR WAX, BOGIES, NAVEL FLUFF
AND DANGLE BERRIES.
SAFE, EFFECTIVE, AS USED BY THE ENTIRE
ROYAL HOUSEHOLD AND SEVERAL
MAJOR PHYSICIANS

GREAT MOMENTS IN HISTORY

MISS EMELIA SRUNGE, THE
FIRST KNOWN VICTIM OF
KILLER BUTTERFLIES

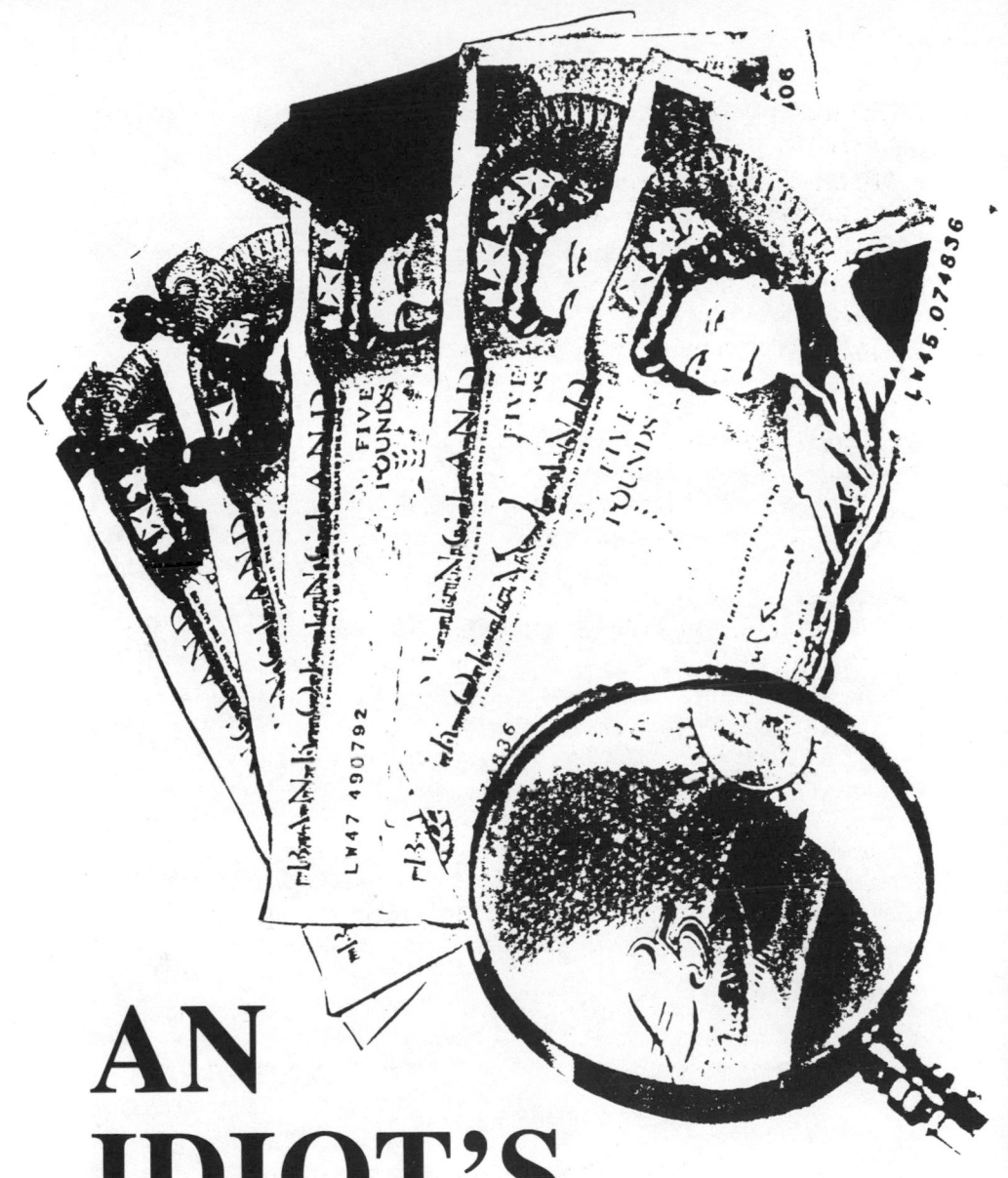

AN
IDIOT'S
GUIDE TO
ECONOMICS

Chaucer's Pardoner, probably the first Thatcherite in English Literature tells us

My theme is alwey oon and evere was,
Radix malorum est Cupiditas.

This has passed into common English usage as **Money is the root of all evil** which is not an accurate translation. It should read **Greed is the root of all evil.**

Money of course can't be the root of anything since it exists usually as bits of metal or paper or plastic that are shifted round from person to person.

Money doesn't do anything.

Money doesn't mug you for example.

People aren't frightened of walking down dark streets at night in case a ten pound note leaps out at them and garrottes them.

You don't hear the newsboys shouting *'Read orl abaht it. Man beaten to death by fifty pence piece!!!'*

No, you get mugged by other people who are after your money.

(In the 1850s, by the way, a man called James Idiot came up with a very interesting theory.

In a letter to *The Times* he wrote . . .

The Theory of Exploding Money by James Idiot
'Dear Sirs,
I submit to those of your readers who find their nightly perambulations undertaken with emotions of fear and misgiving on account of the numbers of footpads and pickpockets that lurk nightly in the alleyways and thoroughfares of our metropolis, that there is in truth a way to facilitate the removal of these brigands from our cities.

I am at the present moment patenting an invention which I have the temerity to call 'Idiot's Exploding Money Device.'

By means of an arrangement of cogs and eccentric cams, pow-ered solely by the new mediums of mesmerism and electricity, my invention inserts a small explosive charge into coins of the realm.

When thus primed the coins are quite safe until taken out of the rightful owner's care; when, after an interval of ten and one half seconds they explode with the force of a small mortar or grenade.

I have tried this device out with great success upon some of my servants and can report that it is extremely efficacious. I respect-fully submit that if all money was made as per 'Idiot's Patent Exploding Money Device' so that it exploded ten and one half seconds after theft from its rightful owner, muggers would soon learn the folly of their ways.'

Idiot was himself arrested and charged with manslaughter after getting his money mixed up and blowing up a lavender girl, three muffin men and a hansom cab driver with his exploding coinage.

However back to the subject. Many people feel that Economics is an extremely complicated subject.

Not at all, Economics is very easy to understand.

Economics is basically about understanding how Man and Money fit together or don't do, whatever the case may be. So basically Economics is the study of Greed.

Before Money, when people wanted things, they just hit each other on the head and took them.

Then somebody invented Money and people just hit each other on the head and took that.

People say that money can't buy happiness, well I've got news for you, neither can poverty; you've got to strike a happy medium as the nun said hitting the grinning clairvoyant.

MONEY

Everybody wants money because money is useful.

With it you can buy things from bread and shoes to yachts and nuclear power stations.

What you get depends on what you pay.

'There are no free lunches,' Friedman's Law.

'He always was a tight bastard,' Friedman's Mother-in-Law.

THE FLOW OF MONEY

You get money for working and then somebody takes it off you so that you can live. This is called *The Flow of Money*

WORK AS WEALTH

In primitive societies a man or woman spends at least a third of his or her life working in the fields or gathering food. The rest of their time is off and they don't do anything other than sit around and sing songs and play with the children and talk to the old people and have fun. This is the sign of a primitive society.

In modern consumer society men and women spend a third of their daily life earning money to buy food and most of the rest of it worrying about how they're going to earn enough money to buy time-saving machines like washers and hoovers that give them the time to go to work to earn more money to buy more time-saving machines. They never see the children and the old people are put in homes. This is the sign of an advanced society.

WAGES

At one time people were not paid wages, they were serfs or slaves and had to work hard just to live. They didn't have CDs or videos or foreign holidays.

Then along came wages. With wages you can afford all those things and only have to work fifty weeks a year for fifty years or until you die, whichever comes sooner.

THE CAPITAL BASE

In Western Society most workers earn a surplus beyond their needs.

After bread and shoes and melon balls there is usually enough left to pay the mortgage.

The mortgage is a system whereby a house worth say twenty thousand pounds eventually costs you forty thousand pounds and on the day you finish paying the mortgage you drop dead and leave it to your children who don't give a bugger about you anyway because you were never there but were always out working to pay off the mortgage.

DISPOSABLE INCOME

Nothing to do with exploding money, this is basically the amount you have left after all necessities have been taken care of, a sort of grown ups' pocket money. Usually just about enough for some bread and half a circus.

MARKET FORCES

A glib phrase that covers up the activities of spies, crooks and chancers.

INFLATION

This is when the cost of things rises faster than the ability of people to pay for them.

DEFLATION

This is when wages go down so much that people can't afford to pay for them.

WORLD MARKET

What you do with your stuff when you've made it. It's no use trying to sell me a washing machine if I make them so therefore you have to destroy my washing machine industry by undercutting me through the employment of slave labour (cf. wages), then when my washing machine industry is destroyed I have to buy your machines.

Alternatively, if I am a third world country, you can take my raw materials for knock-down prices and manufacture them into goods which you then sell back to me. The British Empire was founded on this principle.

COMMUNISM AND CAPITALISM

Are really two sides of the same coin since both suppose that the world is full of endless resources and can be exploited for ever. The only difference is that Capitalism and Communism argue about who owns what, which will seem an academic argument in

a hundred years' time when we're all living in deserts surrounded by poisonous seas.

I mean it doesn't ultimately matter whether the nuclear installation that melted down and gave you cancer was Communist or Capitalist – does it?

Doctor . . . 'I'm afraid you're dying Mr. Soames. But I'm sure you'll be glad to know that it was British Radiation that did it. None of that foreign muck.'

THE GREAT CRASH OF '87

I was half-way to Mt Everest Base Camp at a place called Namche Bazar when I heard about the great Stock Market Crash of the autumn of 1987 and rolled about in the snow for half an hour laughing at the thought of all the yuppies flicking through the pages of their Filofaxes looking for instructions on how to jump out of windows (a dying art since the great crash of the twenties).

I don't want to sound smug or wise after the event but a child could have predicted what would happen and it was all on account of the jam hoarders of Billericay.

You see stocks and shares are really based on little other than confidence in the market. Buying a lot of shares in a company doesn't mean that company is going to perform any better – it only means that you hope it will and have enough confidence in your beliefs to stash your loot in Consolidated Toothpicks or Designer Trusses PLC or wherever it is you've put it.

With so much (or in this case so little) money floating around rumours and insider dealing can cause all sorts of hiccups and fluctuations in the market. Compound this by computerising the whole process adding to the cock-up factor by 30 points on the Richter scale and you have the perfect recipe for disaster on a grand scale.

Now the ladies of the Women's Institute in Billericay are famous for their jams. Each year at the Harvest Sale in the Village Hall gallons and gallons of jams and jellies are sold over the trestle tables in aid of the Dry Rot in the Scout Hut Fund.

For years dealers from all over Europe, the States and even Japan have been coming to Billericay and buying up as much of the famous Marmalade, Ginger and Rhubarb Jam, Redcurrant Jelly and Gooseberry and Mint Preserve that they could get their hands on.

They would take them back to their clients who would lay them down in their cellars as a hedge against inflation.

(A 1927 Wortleberry £20,000 at Sotheby's this very year.)

But in 1987 something strange happened. The entire stock of preserves was bought by a mystery buyer for an undisclosed sum twenty-four hours before the sale.

Rumours flew.

'Aliens Buying Our Jam!!' said a headline in the *Sunday Sport*.

In a desperate bid to get a toehold in the world market, buyers rushed over to Much Dangle in Suffolk and bought up the entire Brownie Camp Fund's Apple and Cinnamon Jelly.

The price of jam spiralled.

People began selling Consolidated Mud and Bacchus Liver Salts, to slam their loot into Ecclefechan Blaeberry and Mealie Puddings PLC and The Eccles Jam Foundry.

'Buy Jam!!!' was the scream around the City as panic buying sent share values through the roof.

But nature abhors a vacuum, and the hole created by panic buying was soon filled by panic selling when rumour went round that the real reason people were jumping out of firms like

97

Consolidated Mud and GKN Fat Renderers was that such firms were going bust.

The well known 'helter skelter' or 'rats from the *Titanic*' effect then took hold. Within hours planes full of fat men with suitcases full of green and crinkly were winging their way to the Leeward Islands while the pavements of London and New York were knee deep in discarded Filofax and the streets were clogged with shirtless yuppies selling Porsches for a fiver apiece.   •

The rest as they say is History.

NEXT WEEK:
HOW TO MAKE A MILLION POUNDS FROM OLD JAM JARS!
HOW TO TURN THOSE SPARE RELATIVES INTO CASH!
ALL IN NEXT MONTH'S WONDERFUL PRACTICAL GREED!

SAFE SEX FOR SWIMMERS

1. Foreplay

2. The Climax

3. Time for a cigarette

Just three of the thousands of detailed instructional illustrations for swimmers in this handy waterproof volume. Essential for anybody involved in water sports. All surface and underwater positions demonstrated. Accompanying video also available.

Not suitable for non-swimmers.

a GIRL IN FOCUS

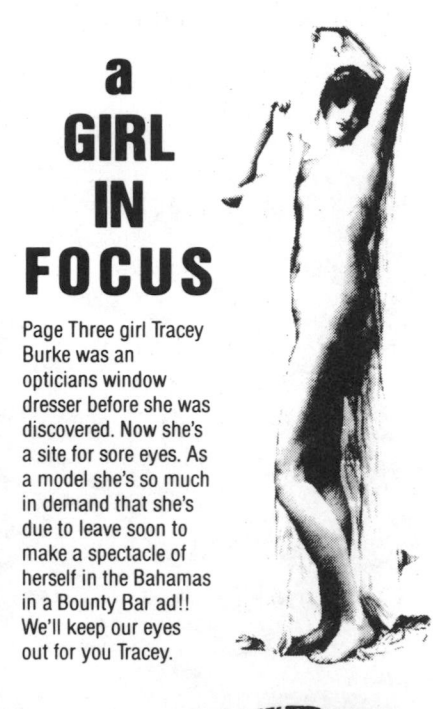

Page Three girl Tracey Burke was an opticians window dresser before she was discovered. Now she's a site for sore eyes. As a model she's so much in demand that she's due to leave soon to make a spectacle of herself in the Bahamas in a Bounty Bar ad!! We'll keep our eyes out for you Tracey.

THE WAGES OF SIN!
TOO MUCH SEX DESTROYED THIS
EX-BISHOP'S LIFE!

'COME ON KIDS MAKE YOUR MINDS UP!' SNARLED
BLACK JAKE. 'WHAT D'YE WANT FER DINNER –
BEAR OR INJUN?'

'THAT'S THE LAST TIME YOU LIGHT YOUR
FARTS IN HERE, ROBINSON' SAID JONES, REACHING
FOR THE FIRE EXTINGUISHER.

TESTING THE CONDOM

TESTING CONDOMS IN
SHAKESPEARE'S ENGLAND

"We're onto something really big here"
Maltravers told the Professor.

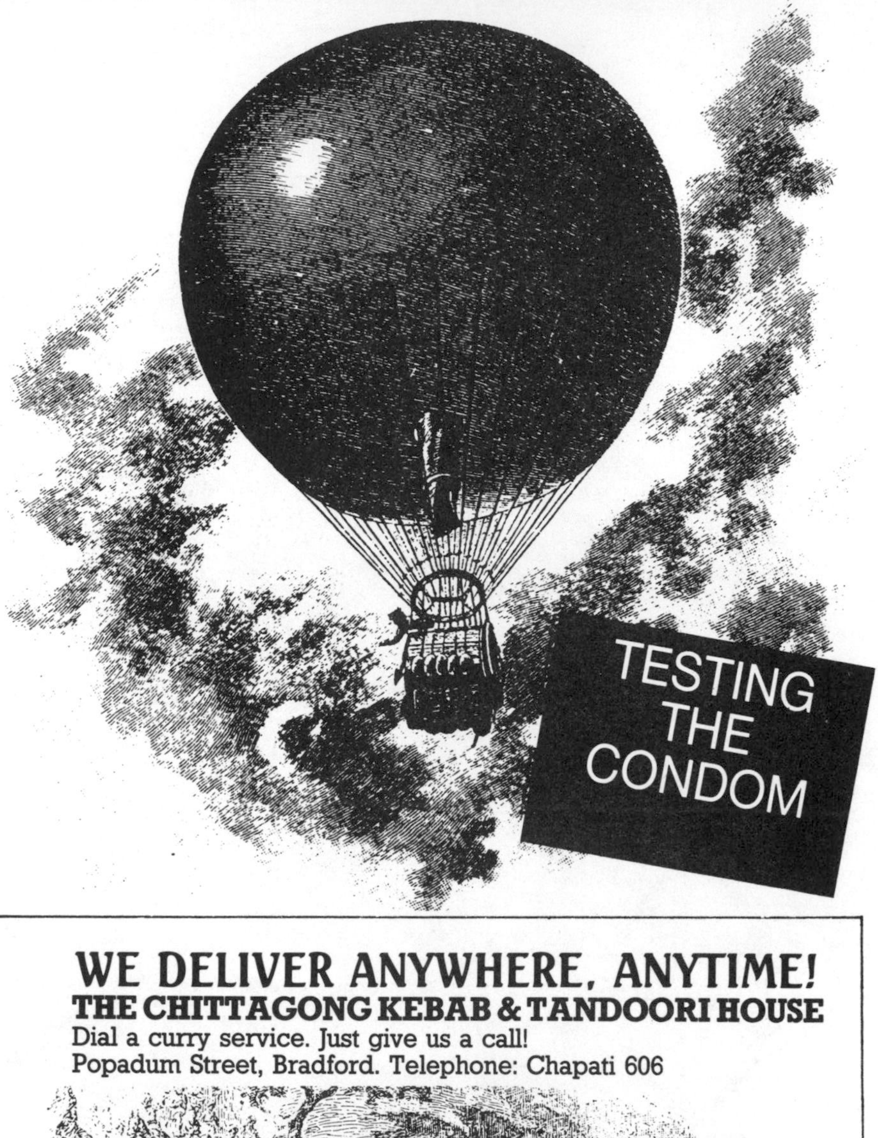

TESTING
THE
CONDOM

WE DELIVER ANYWHERE, ANYTIME!
THE CHITTAGONG KEBAB & TANDOORI HOUSE
Dial a curry service. Just give us a call!
Popadum Street, Bradford. Telephone: Chapati 606

At the sign
of the
steaming
Turban!

TESTING THE CONDOM

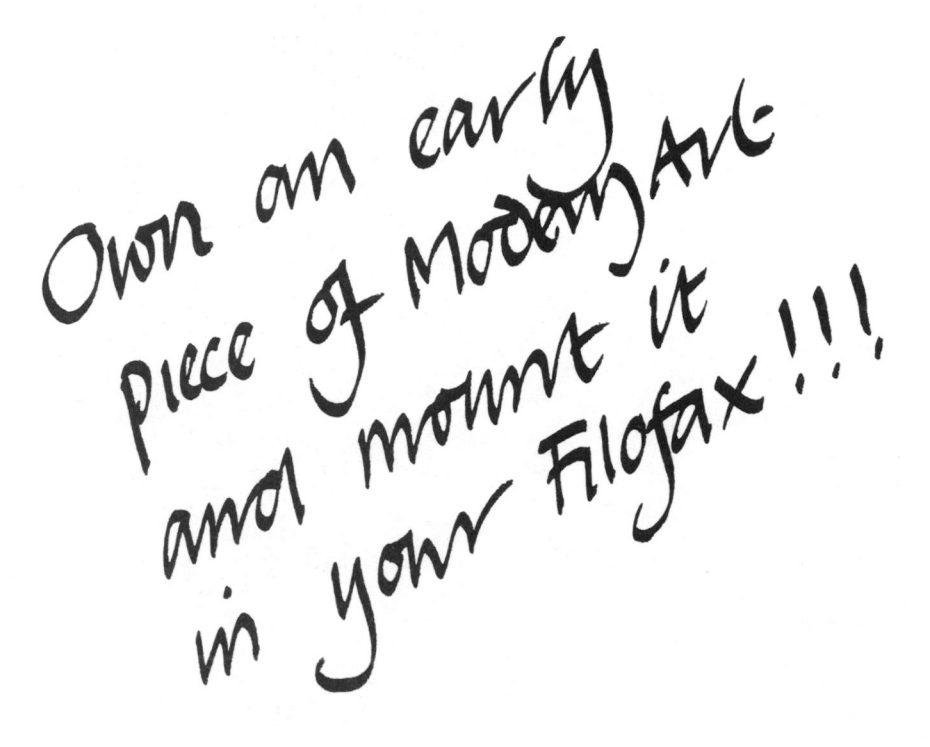

Own an early piece of Modern Art and mount it in your Filofax!!!

HOW TO MOUNT THIS BOOK IN YOUR FILOFAX

You've probably noticed that your Filofax has metal rings on it that go through holes in the paper enabling you to keep all those interesting and necessary things like lists of the great years for French wines and maps of the London Underground, together and yet apart.

Below is a template of a hole.

○

Using the template draw six such holes on the page of the book you wish to mount in your Filofax.

Make the holes with something pointed. (No silly billies – not that!!) Mount the page in your Filofax and trim to size.

6/10 Very good Vincent but haven't we forgotten something?

VINCENT

8/10 very good Toulouse !

LAUTREC

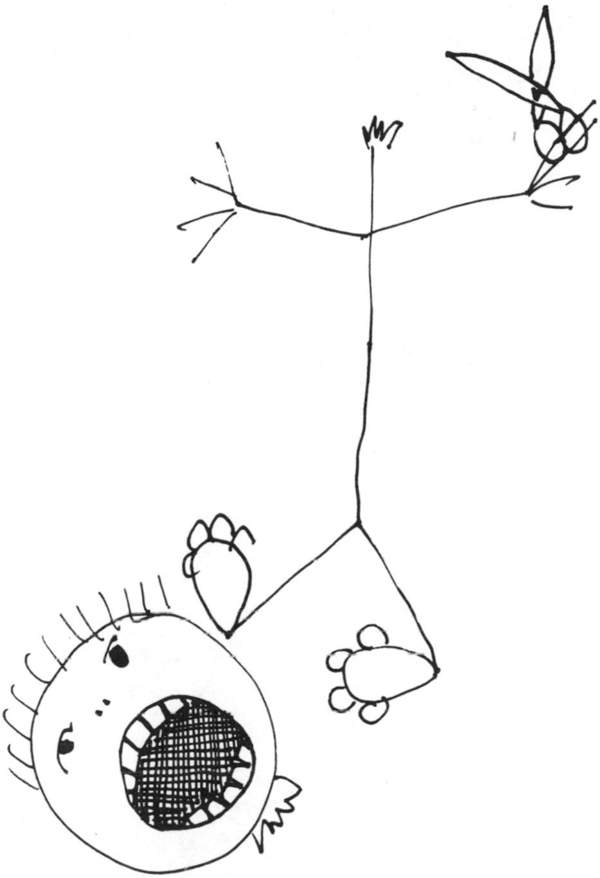

$\frac{0}{10}$

The psychiatrist is coming on Monday Francis!

bacon

110

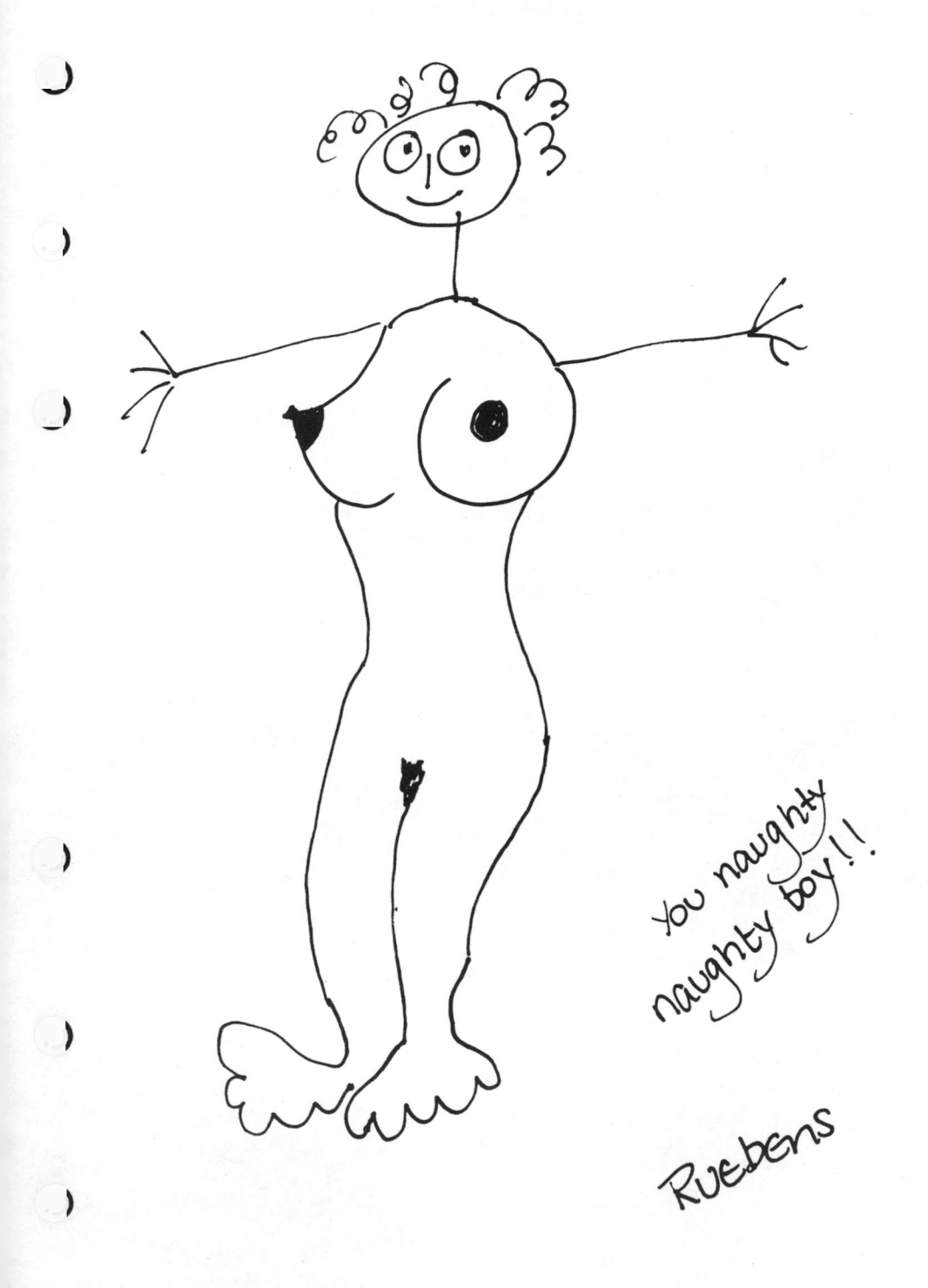

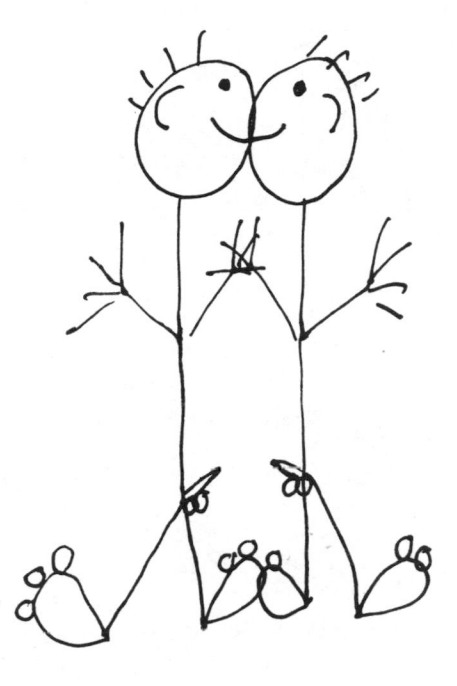

Hockney

%10
David!
See me!
(and bring Jonathan
with you!!)

pollок

% See me!!

Great Moments in History

The Old Roman Sport of Catching the Alsation

114

"Drop that loaded condom" hissed Carruthers

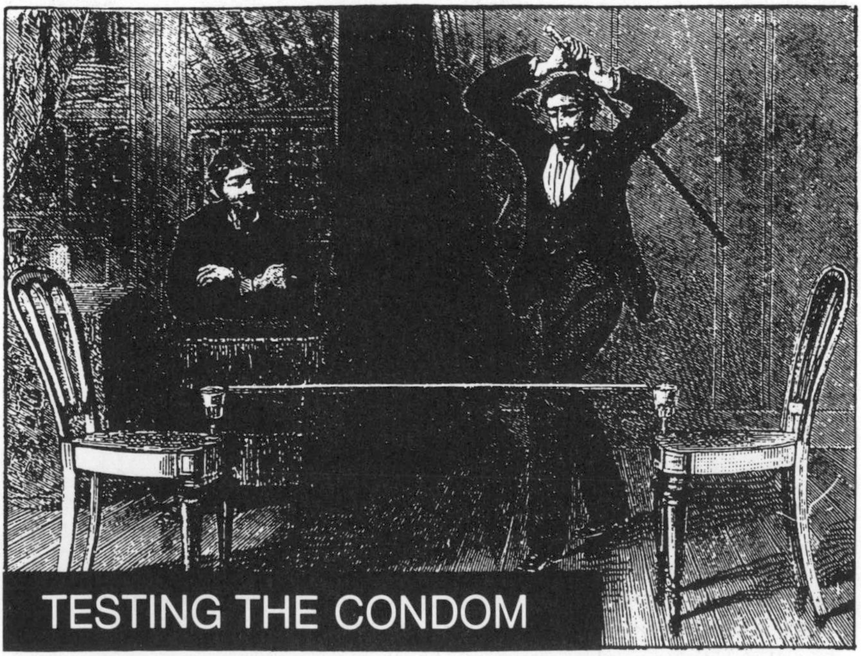

TESTING THE CONDOM

'THIS CAN ONLY MEAN ONE THING' HISSED
MALTRAVERS – 'THE LITLE CHEF IS FURTHER
THAN WE THOUGHT

A LITTLE KNOWN SAINT

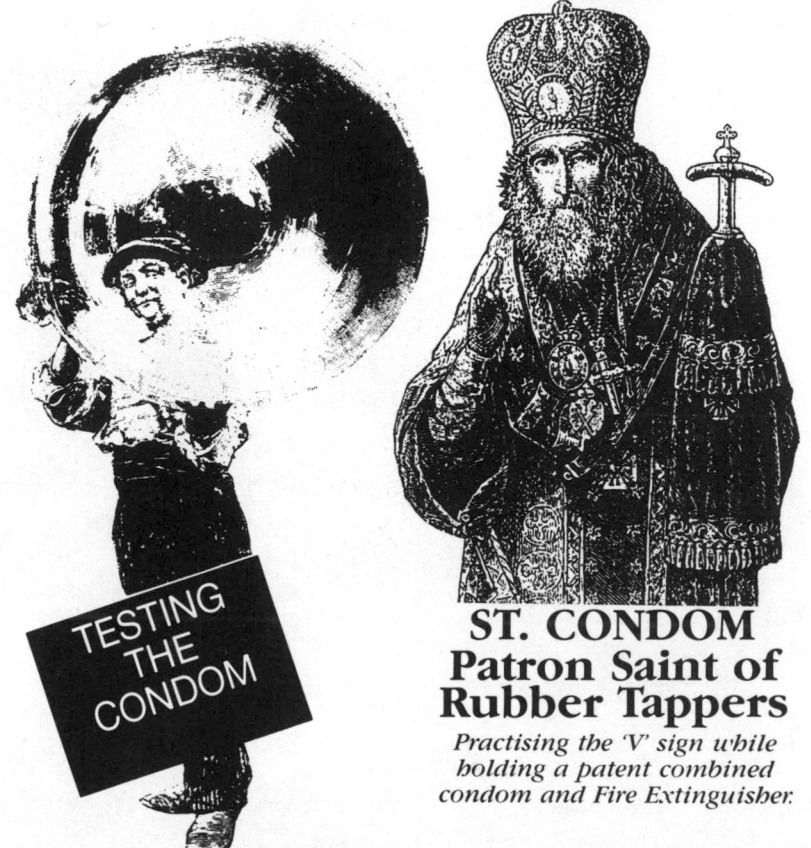

ST. CONDOM
Patron Saint of Rubber Tappers

Practising the 'V' sign while holding a patent combined condom and Fire Extinguisher.

TESTING THE CONDOM

GREAT MOMENTS FROM HISTORY

The Gummer twins demonstrate the success of their cartilage operation.

117

SON OF
THE REVENGE OF
THE RETURN OF
THE KILLER CONDOMS
FROM HELL

PART THREE

SON OF THE REVENGE OF THE RETURN OF THE KILLER CONDOMS FROM HELL

A PLUCKY TALE FOR BOYS

WRITTEN BY MARK HIDING

BASED ON THE FILMS OF MICHAEL WIENER

CAST
Dick Sideboard
Stinker
Dr Evilbugger
Scrotum, his manservant
Aureole, his evil woman assistant
Inspector Thickbastard
Sergeant Densepillock

CHAPTER ONE

THE KNOCKING AT THE DOOR

Dick Sideboard closed the door of the office behind him gently. In front of him, asleep in his chair, one of his cigarettes still burning in his fingers, was his boy assistant Stinker.

'You'll stunt your growth my young man,' hissed Dick in Stinker's ear.

The young tec shot to his feet, a startled expression on his chirpy features.

'Cor lumme, stripe me pink guvnor!' he gulped. 'You put the wind up me then, boss. I must 'ave nodded orf or sumfink.'

Dick smiled.

There was a knock.

He smiled again.

There was another knock.

I must get these loose dentures fixed he thought to himself.

'Someone's at the door, boss,' hissed Stinker.

'Come in!!!' Dick hissed loudly.

The door opened with a crash and a strikingly full-figured, blond woman of an interesting age strode purposefully into the room dressed in a gold lamé sheath dress sprayed on her curvaceous figure, her long hair sweeping majestically behind her as she crossed the room.

Stinker stared open-mouthed as fly buttons shot across the room.

Fly buttons shot across the room

The woman looked at Dick keenly.

He smiled at her appreciatively.

She sat on the desk confidently.

Dick looked at her knowingly.

She opened a silver cigarette case deliberately.

Dick offered her a light puzzledly.

She looked up at him mysteriously.

He stared back quizzically.

'One of us had better say something soon or the writer's going to run out of adverbs,' said Dick warmly and cheerfully but not too informally.

The blond stood up to her full height of eight foot six and three-quarters and in a deep husky voice like the noise of walnut shells being cracked with a jackboot said

'My name is Count Von Tooten.'

He clicked his high heels together and saluted wildly, his massive, red-fingernailed hand crashing into his bouffant hair like a downed, hairy, pink zeppelin.

'Luscious Lena to base'

122

'Lumme Guv. The broad's a geezer,' croaked Stinker amazedly.

The count pulled up his amply filled sweater, unscrewed the end of one of his brassiere cups and pulled out a small microphone.

'Luscious Lena to base,' he called into the microphone. 'I've made contact with the subject and am about to proceed as per orders over.'

There was a crackling noise from the other cup of the brassiere and a tinny, reedy voice said,

'Listen Jimmy when you've picked up that fare can you call at the Taj Mahal and pick up a chicken tandoori with nan bread and an extra portion of madras sauce and a prawn vindaloo off the bone with four popadums and two chapatis.'

'Bloody taxi cabs,' muttered the Count thumping himself on the bust frustratedly.

'What's going on?' asked Dick. 'Who the hell are you and what the blazes are you doing here? And what am I doing swearing like this in a boys' comic?'

'A fleet of giant Condoms has destroyed New York!' said the Count staring Dick full in the face.

'You don't mean . . . .' Dick began.

'Yes I do' said the Count, 'this could mean the beginning of civilisation as we know it!'

CHAPTER TWO
TO THE LIGHTHOUSE

My name is Orlando and i shouldn't really be in this novel at all since by rights i belong to Virginia Woolf but i'm really hacked off with being in her book because there's bugger all going on and taking a long time about it too you see it's all on account of this stream of consciousness thing which if you ask me is a load of lord mayor's bollix because after all is anybody really interested in every single thought a character has? i mean i was talking to Leopold Bloom the other day as he was frying some kidneys over the fire and he told me that Stephen Dedalus never thought those

things about the snot-green, scrotum-tightening sea at all that was all James Joyce's doing because he had a cold on account of the damp in that Trieste flat and had trouble with his undercarriage on account of Nora spending most of the housekeeping on hats meaning he i.e. James had to wear cheap y-fronts

Anyway what i am doing is waiting for a lift in Dick Sideboards car so i can get to Hanging Gulch and get a part in a Zane Grey cowboy story which is what a boy of my age should be in and not one of those bloody boring Bloomsbury writers' books – gets right on my tit ends does all that stuff i want campfires, cowboy songs, stampedes, dead indians and a Mexican friend called Flaco whose sister is dark and luscious and who i serenade with a guitar under the wide bowl of stars and whose knickers come down in Chapter Eleven.

Just a minute there's a noise

It must be them

The last thing that went past was Pooh Bear and all his pillocky friends i feel sorry for that Christopher Robin trapped in there with all them bloody crazy animals making Pooh sticks and throwing them in the river bloody big deal wait till i throw my leg over that young Mexican lady – you can stuff your pooh sticks then!

Yes it's them i can hear the car engine

Bugger me! it's a Hispano Suiza!

CHAPTER THREE
ORLANDO HITCHES A LIFT

The Hispano Suiza snarled to a halt, clouds swirling round it in the dusty road.

'Does Mrs Woolf know you're out?' asked Dick, opening the door for him to jump in.

'She's gone to Lytton Strachey's house for a country weekend. They'll all be walking round drinking home-made flower wine talking about William Morris and jumping in and out of bed with each other.'

'Sounds fine to me guv,' said Stinker putting down his by now almost rigid copy of Health and Efficiency.

'You wouldn't like it Stinker. It's full of intellectual women wearing hand-woven clothes and roman sandals. They spend most of their time coming and going and talking of Michelangelo – they have a special room for it. When they're not doing that they're either running away from H. G. Wells or trying to get into bed with him.'

He put his foot down and the great beast leaped forward shooting through the country lanes like a six cylinder, forty eight horse-power frog.

a six cylinder, forty eight horse-power frog

In the back the Count dozed fitfully. Dick had learned from him all he needed to know about the strange and fearful events of the past few days.

Apparently a fleet of Giant inter-stellar condoms had appeared above New York. At first people had laughed thinking it was a publicity stunt for Mates. But then when one of the condoms had destroyed the Empire State Building while another had flattened the Museum of Modern Art people had begun to realise that, if this was a publicity stunt, it had gone way over the top.

In four hours the entire city had been razed to the ground and everybody in it wiped out.

The Count worked for the World Intelligence Logistics Laboratory Inc. – WILLI for short – the greatest think-tank in the world. The same brains that had given us the Hula Hoop, the Gonk and those rotten-hard puzzles with tiny ball bearings that you have to get into stupid little holes that end up being thrown across the room on wet Sunday afternoons.

WILLI was recruiting the best brains in the world in an attempt to save it from destruction by the condoms which, research had shown, came from outer space.

Now the two tecs and the Count were speeding south to WILLI's secret headquarters to meet with other great brains and work out a solution that could save the world.

After what seemed to Orlando like hours but was in fact only a page and a half, the Hispano Suiza pulled off the road at the town limits of Hanging Gulch letting Orlando out. They waved goodbye to him, watching his diminutive figure approach the main street.

He had almost reached the town when an Apache arrow slashed through his neck rendering him lifeless.

'Going to be a short book that,' said Dick driving on.

'What is, boss?' asked Stinker, his intellect burning feebly inside his psyche like a candle in a damp meat cellar.

'*Riders of the Alkali Trail* by Virginia Woolf,' hissed Dick smiling.

'Going to be a short book that', said Dick

As night began to fall the travellers saw ahead of them a light burning intermittently, high across the far moors.

'That is the headquarters of WILLI' hissed the Baron.

'They are expecting us.'

Shortly after the three chums were sitting in the control room deep in the bowels of the Earth sipping their hot cocoa. The Count crossed his legs. His pink nylon rabbit slippers waggled their ears in the fire's glow. Stinker nodded off gently, a copy of Big and Bouncy slipping from his hand. Dick stared into the fire.

Yes they were definitely flames.

The door opened.

'Major General Bent,' proclaimed a voice. Attached to it was a husky frame topped with an enormous ginger moustache and the shining dome of a pink bald head. The face was so red and choleric that the eyes and mouth were mere pinpricks in it while the nose was squashed into the face like a cigar butt stubbed in a bowl of dough – a souvenir of too many inter-services boxing tournaments.

His head looks like a flying dumpling, thought Dick.

His head looks like a navel orange being attacked by a brush, thought Stinker.

I wonder if the young chap goes? thought the General.

I wonder what all this wondering is about? thought the Count.

'Follow me' said the General imperiously, adding 'and watch the stairs. I nearly put my back out this morning. They're awful slippy. Gave it a right twist I did. I saw stars I can tell you. Ooh the pain! It shot all the way from here to here. I felt proper nauseous, I did!'

That nail varnish doesn't suit his colouring, thought Dick.

The General led them even further into the bowels of the Earth along corridor after corridor. They could hear a constant humming as though of a mighty machine.

'Is that constant humming the humming of a mighty machine?' asked Dick.

'Yes! and doesn't it get on your wick!' replied the General. 'I tell you what. You listen to that all day and you don't half get a woolly head. What with that and these flowrescent choobes it doesn't half bring my migraine on, I can tell you.'

After a few more miles of endless corridor and bitching the chums found themselves at the nerve centre of a mighty Empire.

A vast room filled from floor to ceiling with screens and dials. Cathode ray tubes glowed and all sorts of interesting looking things made beeping and whirring noises. (*I don't know what they were – I'm not an electronics engineer!!*)

'Shouldn't we skip the next chapter and get into our space suits so we can be shot into space to find out where these Giant Killer Condoms are coming from that have destroyed every major city in the world except Birmingham which they thought was destroyed already?' asked Dick. 'This story is taking for ever!'

'Okay,' beamed a mad scientist who has a walk-on part in this tale and who now disappears for ever into the far off land of Booktenstein.

CHAPTER FOUR
THEY SKIP A CHAPTER

CHAPTER FIVE
INTO THE BLACK HOLE

The three chums crawled out of the far side of Chapter Four and stood beneath the giant star ship that was to transport them into the depths of Outer Space.

'I'll 'ave ter go back boss,' croaked Stinker. 'I've left me copy of Big and Bouncy in Chapter Four. I know exactly where it is. It's on top of a paragraph near the bottom of the page.'

'Ve haf no time,' said the Count reverting to type. 'I yam haffink to speek like dis to make my character more interesting. Gut Ya? Now we are haffink to gets into ze flyink machine and varoom she will go!'

This is going to be be bloody painful, thought Dick. If I have to listen to this camp Kraut spouting bad Ealing Comedy German for the next two light years I'm getting out of this book.

They climbed the shining ladder into the giant tube.

'Ve vill ze safety belts have to fasten,' offered the Count.

They clipped in and looked about them. The control panel was blank, there was no steering wheel, no dials, no flashing lights; just a red button that said **'GO'** in capital letters.

'Cor lumme! Stripe me pink guv!' hissed Stinker. 'There's nuffink to steer wiv!'

'It's OK man stay cool!' hissed Dick. 'The writer knows where we're going.'

'Why are you talking funny boss?' asked Stinker.

'If the Kraut can do it so can I! Here's looking at yer kid. Play it again Sam. Get off yer horse and drink yer milk.'

They climbed the shining ladder into the giant tube.

Stinker stood up and opened a door in the back of the control room. He closed it again and whistled softly to himself. There in front of him on a large fur rug that took up most of the room was the most beautiful woman Stinker had ever seen. Naked but for her clothes she beckoned Stinker towards her.

'What are you doing here?' croaked Stinker, fly buttons ricocheting off the wall.

'The writer sent me,' she crooned soothingly, her rose red lips puckering deliciously. 'He's never written anybody like me before. I'm a stock character.'

And she let her flimsy clothes slip to the floor. I think.

'I'm Dr. Evilbugger's assistant. He's the brains behind all this.'

Stinker gulped to give the writer time to work out what happens next.

'You've killed a hundred and twenty million people already and plot to take over the whole universe!!!'

She waggled her bosoms at him.

'Mind you, that doesn't make you a bad person,' whispered Stinker. 'And you can always make a Perfect Act of Contrition.'

Just then the door burst open. It was Dick.

'Stinker, you're needed on the bridge!!' he hissed.

'But guvnor . . .' moaned Stinker.

'It's no good Stinker. He's writing her out of the plot. She's too hot for him to handle. His wife's getting suspicious. She thinks he's spending too much time at the typewriter – keeps findin' ink on his collar.'

Stinker groaned woefully. Then, turning back to say goodbye noticed that the room was empty. All trace of the woman and the fur rug had been erased.

'And he never even wrote in the roaring log fire and the glasses of sparkling red German wine from the Moselle.' whined Stinker.

'You can't have a roaring log fire on a space ship, you pratt!!' hissed Dick.

'Well, he could 'ave tried.' muttered the frustrated young tec dejectedly.

Back in the control room the Count was preparing for take-off. He put the hand-mirror back in his purse and pressed his lips together on a Kleenex to take off the excess lipstick.

'You are ready, nein?' he demanded.

They nodded.

The Count leaned forward and pressed the button. With a roar the space craft leaped into the sky.

Up into the heavens it sped leaving the Earth a tiny blue- green speck beneath them.

'Farewell plucky little planet,' thought Dick. 'Let's hope that we can save you after all.'

Around them gathered the inky blackness of the universe, a vast indigo cloak spattered with an infinity of stars. Other suns, other worlds. Everywhere children were being put to bed, lovers were gazing up at the stars, walkers out on the common were staring skywards looking at the great bowl of night, little knowing the drama that was being enacted in those frozen airless wastes.

'Shisse!!!' screeched the Count leaping to his feet. "I haf ze door left open!'

Leaping across the control room he threw himself at the door. Outside the stars spun past. He struggled to close it but it was too late. The cat ran straight between his legs and fell twenty thousand feet landing safely not far from its home. Unfortunately, while crossing the road it was run over by a fish van and flattened. Ironic, isn't it?

The door clanged shut and the Count sat down.

'Shisse!!' he said. 'Now ve vill by ze mouses be over-ranned.'

'Run,' corrected Dick.

'Vere to?' asked the Count.

'Watch out,' shouted Stinker, but it was too late. While nobody had been watching, including the author, the space craft had been drawn into one of the deadliest known of space phenomena. A Black Hole!

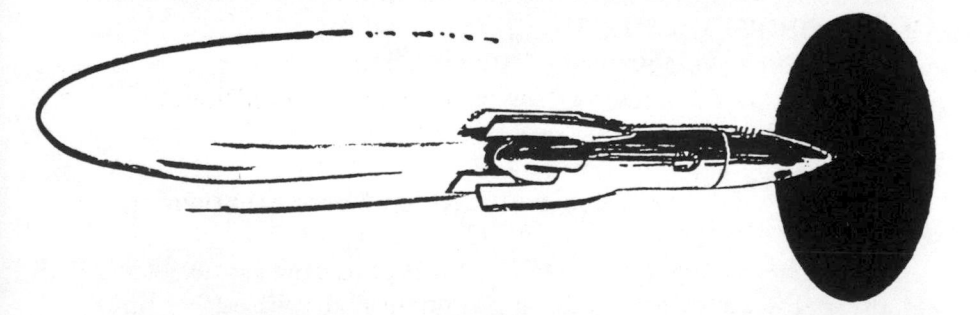

Down the giant spacecraft tumbled, sucked into that terrible vortex until, one by one, the three chums lost consciousness.

CHAPTER SIX

TRAPPED ON THE PLANET OF THE LITTLE TADPOLE THINGS THAT LOOK LIKE SPERMS!!!

The three chums awoke to find themselves chained to three steel tables and wearing only their underwear. Above them bright lights burned fiercely and around them stood hundreds of strange tadpole-like creatures.

'Ooobledy boobledy' said one of the creatures raising his hand.

'Ooobledy boobledy' chanted all the others. Two of the creatures stepped forward and untied the chums who stood groggily rubbing their cramped limbs.

'Why did you bring us here?' asked Dick.

'Oobledy boobledy,' answered the largest of the creatures who, by his size and air of importance, Dick took to be the leader.

'Vot ze fork zis 'ooble boobedley' mean?' asked the Count scratching his head.

Dick switched on his translatathon.

'Why have you brought us here?' he asked again.

'OOOOBLY DOOBLEDY!!!!' screeched the creature.

'What did he say guv?' asked Stinker.

'I knew it would come to this,' said Dick wearily. 'They want us to teach them the Okey Cokey.'

He stood before the throne of the king of the Giant Sperms and, knowing their very lives depended on it, he taught them the Okey Cokey.

They learned quickly and within half an hour the hundreds of Giant Sperm were dancing up and down and in and out waving their bits about like foetal morris dancers.

'You put your left leg in
Your left leg out

In, out, in, out,
Shake it all about' sang Dick.

KNOWING THEIR VERY LIVES DEPENDED
ON IT DICK SLOWLY TAUGHT THE GIANT
SPERMS THE OKEY COKEY

Suddenly he hissed out of the corner of his mouth 'Quick chaps our only hope is to make a dash for it!'

While the Giant Sperm were putting their whole fronts in and shaking them about the three chums scooted across the floor of the throne room. They had almost made the door when a huge net fell from the ceiling trapping them completely. Their hopes of escape were dashed and the Count's coiffeur was ruined foerever.

'Oobledy boobledy' said the king.

'Bollocks!' said Dick.

The three chums were marched out of the throne room and down a long corridor filled with machinery. The Giant Sperms trotted by their side obbledy boobledying.

'The fiends!!' thought Stinker.

They were taken into a large room where loose fitting unfashionable oversuits were thrust at them.

They mustn't like the look of our underwear thought Dick.

'I aint wearin' this, it's years out of fashion!' moaned Stinker.

'Ooobledy Doobledy' said one of the Giant Sperm.

'*Factories, Offices and Workshops Act,* Stinker! They're only doing their jobs.' said Dick consolingly.

On they went, deep into the bowels of the planet.

'What's that smell Guvnor?' asked Stinker.

'We're in the bowels of the planet.' hissed Dick.

'That's a rotten joke Guvnor' groaned Stinker.

'The writers running out of ideas.' hissed Dick quite untruthfully.

All around them loomed massive machines, tended by more of the Giant Sperm things, slaves to a mighty evil empire. As he passed the giant machines Dick looked up. Above him great bubbles of latex were being blown into shape by huge funnels making more and more space condoms for the subjugation of the Universe.

Is there no end to their evilness? thought Dick ungrammatically.

They arrived at length in a huge hall where they were chained to three more tables.

'Zis is getting tedious,' said the Count.

Then, as though at a secret command, the three tables slid into the air and across the great room coming to rest above a massive pit.

'IS THERE NO END TO THEIR EVILNESS?'
THOUGHT DICK UNGRAMMATICALLY

Boiling acids seethed in the pit while around it stood a hundred twelve-headed crocodiles with savage teeth, their gaping jaws belching fire. Above the pit a gigantic, fearsome, phantasmagoric, overwritten pendulum swung, razor-sharp, descending a little with each arc until it was only inches above the three plucky chums.

'Cor lumme! Stripe me pink guv! We crapped out this time!' said Stinker.

'You're quiet, Count,' hissed Dick.

'Zere is not much to say yah ven zis forking knife is going to cut mine vedding tackle to bitzes!!! Dumkopf!'

With one leap Dick was free. Using a rare form of halitosis learnt from a Japanese martial arts expert he forced the tadpole things back across the great hall by breathing on them, untying Stinker and the Count as he did so.

'So,' said Dick as they ran down the passageway and out onto the surface of the planet. 'It all makes sense now. We were captured by these tadpole things when they drew us into that black hole. The tadpole things are the builders of the giant condoms and are plotting to destroy the Earth in revenge for . . . . for. . . . for. . . . . '

'For what guv?' asked Stinker.

'In revenge for being little tadpole things,' hissed Dick, his breath coming in pants.

'Zat's a nice pair of trousers which your breath is vearink,' said the Count.

'The atmosphere on this planet is a mixture of cyanide and arsenic,' said Dick. 'Try not to breathe any of it and don't lick your fingers.'

They came to a big hole in the planet's surface.

Suddenly a Giant Condom shot into the sky.

'So that's where they come from!!' hissed Dick as the giant condom soared skywards.

CHAPTER SEVEN
DOOMED AGAIN

'What's that creaking guv?' asked Stinker, looking down into the fearful void.

'SO THAT'S WHERE THEY COME FROM!' HISSED DICK
AS THE GIANT CONDOM SOARED SKYWARDS

'It's the plot, Stinker,' hissed Dick.

Suddenly everything went black.

'Bloody short days on this planet,' muttered Stinker sliding into unconsciousness.

When they came to, they were back in the throne room of the King Sperm.

'Just what is your evil plan?' hissed Dick.

'Ooobledy Boobledy,' said the King Sperm.

'Vot is he sayink?' asked the Count.

'He says they're going to destroy all life in the Universe and people it with their own kind. The entire Cosmos will be full of these little sperm things dancing the Okey Cokey,' Dick translated.

He stuck his chin out.

'Bastards!!' hissed Stinker.

'Svinehund, pig dog shpermatazoa!!' snarled the Count.

'You'll never get away with this!' said Dick.

But they did.

THE END

WHATEVER HAPPENED TO DR. EVILBUGGER?
WHO IS INSPECTOR THICKBASTARD?
DON'T MISS NEXT WEEK'S 'INCREDIBLY BORING STORIES'
PUBLISHED BY
WASTE A FOREST INC.
MICHIGAN
ILLINOIS

TESTING THE CONDOM

ALBERT AND THE
CONDOM

AS PERFORMED BY STANLEY HOLLOWAY

There's a famous seaside place called Morecambe
As is noted for sweet F.A.
And Mr. and Mrs. Ramsbottom went there
With young Albert on t'chara one day.

A right little pillock were young Albert
He were always in trouble tha knows;
He'd firkle about and dismantle a thing
And break it to see how it goes.

Aye a right little wozzak were Albert,
An obnoxious little pratt,
He'd 'ad that many belts from his father
That the top of his head were quite flat.

Now they didn't think much to Morecambe,
It were cold and everywhere were shut.
Pa said 'Fer an August Bank 'Oliday
I think it's a bit bloody much!

And we're booked in here for the whole bloomin' week
Ah'll go piggin' mad in this dump!'
'Look on't bright side' said Mother 'It could have been worse
We could 'ave gone to Skegness for a month.'

Now boardin' 'ouse where they were stayin'
Sunny Seaview Villas it were called.
Front windows looked out on t'gasometer
Back windows on t'slaughterhouse wall.

Landlady had catered for Lucrezia Borgia
She were so tight she counted the salt.
T'mice were picketin' t'kitchen
And t'food were so bad, cat were bald.

On t'first night Mr. and Mrs. Ramsbottom
Left little Albert in on his own,
While they went for a gill in The Pig and Manic Depressive
'Free and Easy With Fred on the Paper and Comb.'

Now Albert had read all t'magazines,
Sunday Sport, Our Own and What's Yours?
So he went upstairs for a firkle about
And started rootin in t'dressin' table drawers.

What 'ee found there were quite amazin'
'Ee never 'ad seen one before.
Night Rider it were called and Albert thought, Night Rider!
It must be summat as you wore!

'Is dad 'ad a crash 'at on t'moped,
'Appen this were smaller only in red.
So t'little lad took it out of t'packet
And rolled it right over 'is 'ead.

When the Ramsbottoms come back at closin' time
Little Albert were nowhere about.
''Appen 'ee's in bed' said Father
''Appen we'll go upstairs and find out.'

Well they found Albert wanderin' round t'landin'
Moanin' and treadin' on t'cat.
''Ee's a condom on 'is 'ead!' said Father.
And Mother said ''Eee fancy that!'

'It's stuck on 'is 'ead!' said Father
''Ee's rolled it right down to 'is neck.
And 'is eyes look like boiled eggs in clingfilm.'
And Mother said 'Ee! I am vexed!

What did you go and do that there for our Albert?
You've got yourself in a right mess!'
And all Albert said was 'Mmmnnnn arggghh mummmf mummmf
Muummmf muummmf nnnnnnng nnnng mnmn mnmn.'

"Ee's going a peculiar colour!' said Father
"Appen 'ee's goin' to die!'
'If 'ee does I'll be vexed' said Mother
'I've just bought 'im that new shirt and tie.'

'We'll 'ave to make an 'ole in it', said Father
"Is voice is gettin right weak.
It's a shame to waste a good condom
But we 'ave paid full board for 'im for t'week.'

So they cut a little hole in the condom
With the saw that they used on the bread.
But tug as they would it were no bloomin' good
It were stuck like gum on 'is 'ead!

T'fire brigade 'ad to be sent for
'I'm proper flippin' blazin' said Dad
'Next time poke a Lion wi' a stick or summat!
We can claim on t'insurance for that!'

Firemen came and soon snipped it away,
Pa gave them a quid for their trouble.
But they were laughing so much they crashed the fire truck
And reduced the Pig and Manic Depressive to rubble.

'All's well that ends well!' said Mother
'That may well be' Father said 'but
It were t'only one left and tomorrow's t'weekend
And t' piggin' chemist is shut!'

THE END

143

Alien Giant Hailstones made Me gay and pregnant Claims Elvis Look alike

WHILE DRIVING THROUGH DEATH VALLEY I CAME ACROSS THE *WEEKLY WORLD NEWS.* I THOUGH IT CONTRIBUTED SO MUCH TO THE ARTISTIC LIFE OF OUR PLANET THAT I DECIDED I WOULD LIKE TO SHARE IT WITH YOU. EVERY WORD, I ASSURE YOU, IS TRUE!

144

Legless, armless dwarf marooned on bar stool

By HENRY WEBER

Handicapped Hugo Cannon spent two hellish hours marooned on a bar stool in an empty tavern!

"It was a nightmare," said Cannon, who was born without arms or legs but generally gets around well with his artificial limbs.

"You can't imagine what it's like to be in a position like that," he added. "If the night watchman hadn't come along when he did I'd still be stranded.

"The bums who propped me up took my artificial arms and legs and I'm helpless without them."

Newspapers said the drama unfolded when Cannon, 26, dropped into Van Gaal's bar in Salzburg, Austria, for a nightcap and struck up a conversation with a pair of strangers.

Things at first were pleasant enough, said the press. But Cannon's new pals soon turned vicious.

"They started teasing me about my deformities and making cracks about my manhood," said Cannon.

"One of them pulled my arms straight off. The other one took my legs."

Cannon's pleas for help apparently went unnoticed in the noisy tavern. One of the strangers eventually shoved a sock into his mouth and balanced him on a stool in a corner. Bartender Willi Ritschel later told police he didn't notice Cannon when he locked up for the night.

In fact, two hours passed before watchman John Tolson found the helpless cripple and notified the cops, who reportedly have two suspects in the case but have not yet been able to locate them.

"You can't understand how cruel this was unless you know Hugo," Sgt. Louis Kruger told reporters.

"He's really one of the nicest little guys you'd ever want to meet."

Cannon added: "It's tough being handicapped under the best of circumstances. But what these guys did really stinks."

Killer's blessing?

Whoever killed 52-year-old Annie Stone attached a sign to her body that read "God bless you, Ma!" Arrested and charged with murder was Stephen Davis — the dead woman's 24-year-old son, Long Island, N.Y., cops report.

145

CORPSE EXPLODES IN THE CASKET

Horrified family flees funeral home after bizarre blast

WEEKLY WORLD 55¢

NEWS

Hubby's suit charges: Wife's chain-smoking makes our kids sick

March 8, 1988   30587   VOL. 9, Issue 22

Incredible new medical discovery!

SNEEZING INCREASES YOUR BUST SIZE

800 women grew by several bra sizes, says doctor after study

REINCARNATION SHOCKER!

My dead wife came back — as a goose!

She eats like a queen on $15 a week!

Couple fights for custody of ghost who picks the horses!

World's meanest boss — he fires his own father!

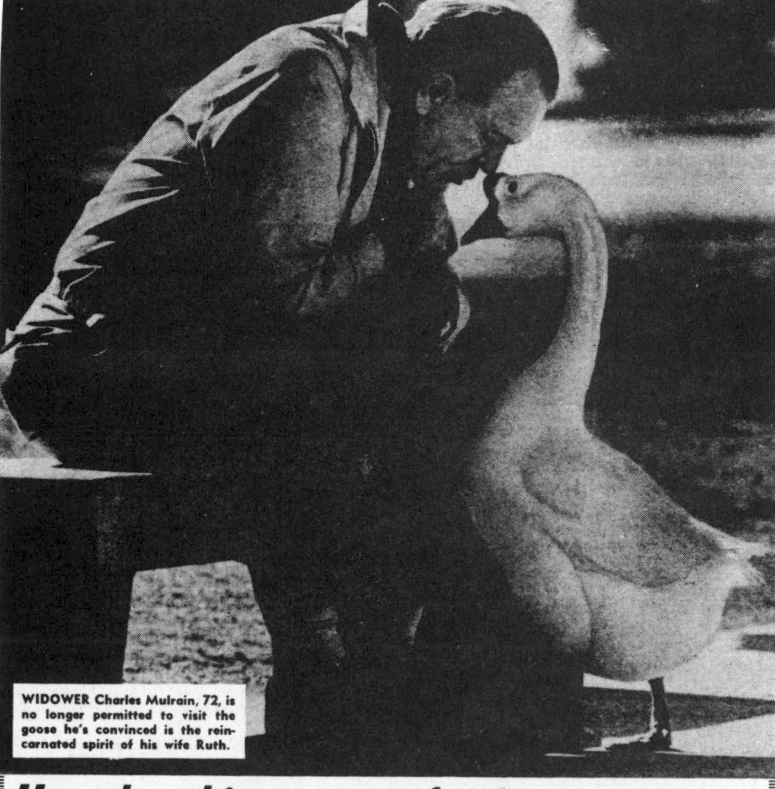

WIDOWER Charles Mulrain, 72, is no longer permitted to visit the goose he's convinced is the reincarnated spirit of his wife Ruth.

Heartbreaking story of reincarnation:

My wife's come back as a goose!

By SUSAN JIMISON

Retiree Charles Mulrain's wife died 13 years ago, but he's convinced she has come back to him again — as a white goose!

The Tucson, Ariz., widower swears his wife Ruth inhabits the elegant bird who visited him daily in a park near his home. And now the 72-year-old former gas worker is in mourning for a second time, because park officials got rid of the goose and no one will tell him where she is.

. . . but her new owners won't let me see her anymore, says lonely retiree

"I'd look in that goose's beautiful blue eyes and I could feel something — my wife was in that goose," Mulrain told The NEWS. "It reminded me of Ruth. I could talk to it.

"The park guards came and took her away right in front of me. I feel like I've lost a connection with my wife for a second time. I used to visit her every day, sometimes twice a day. It's really lonesome over at the park now."

Mulrain first saw the white goose two years ago when he visited Reid Park. The goose adopted him immediately and each time he returned to the park, she greeted him enthusiastically.

"She'd run to dad and greet him. The bird had an attachment to him that reminded him of Mom, who was a very loving wife," said Mulrain's daughter, Mary Spiros.

"The goose would be vicious to other people, but she was very gentle with my dad. She would chase people away from him and protect him."

A few weeks ago, the goose attacked a park visitor during a public fair near the lake. The visitor complained and the goose was taken away to the Humane Society. Mulrain went to visit his feathered friend at the Society and Mrs. Spiros was preparing to adopt it for her dad, when the bird was given to someone else — who won't let Mulrain see the goose anymore.

Mrs. Spiros said her father — who lives alone — never got over his wife's death.

"He still mourns for Mom — now he's grieving for the goose as well."

147

Boy, 16, has never slept, say doctors

WEEKLY WORLD
NEWS
55¢

April 5, 1988   30587   VOL. 9, Issue 26

RE-VOLT-ING!
Wife can't touch her electrified husband

Startling satellite photos confirm . . .

WW2 BOMBER FOUND ON MOON

Perfectly preserved warplane sitting in crater, say experts

★ ★ ★

HE'S B-A-A-A-CK!
600 Hitlers cloned by Russians

Super psychic's pledge: Drop me a line — and I'll tell your future!

★ ★ ★

EXCLUSIVE!
How to be a TV preacher and make big $$

0   710496

He's back — this time there are 600 of them

RUSSIANS CLONING ADOLF HITLERS!

HE ALMOST RULED THE WORLD... and that's why the Russians want to find out what made Adolf Hitler tick.

As many as 600 Adolf Hitlers are alive and well in the Soviet Union, each cloned from a blood-stained handkerchief found in the Fuhrer's pocket after his suicide in 1945!

That's the astonishing claim of Dr. Rudolf Hegeman, who allegedly helped the Soviets clone their army of Hitlers before he suffered a debilitating stroke last year.

"Hitler is alive and his clones will live for generations to come," said the expert. "The Russians have made study of the man a priority.

"They want to understand the psychological and neurological makeup of a man who almost ruled the world."

Soviet officials refused to discuss Dr. Hegeman's allegations and would neither confirm nor deny their accuracy. The expert himself told reporters that Russia's Hitler clones range in age from 6 months to 38 years. When the difference in their ages is taken into account they are virtually identical, he added. All have IQs that fall between 110 and 125.

They also have artistic ability and a powerful charisma though their social skills are definitely lacking.

"We expected the clones to have most of Hitler's characteristics and quirks because they were created from blood cells containing his unique genetic blueprint," said Dr. Hegeman. "There are variations, of course, because the clones have different educations and life experiences. But they essentially are the same man that led Nazi Germany to the brink of world domination before the end of the Second World War."

Historians disagree about the demise of Hitler but it is generally believed that he committed suicide in a Berlin bunker to avoid capture by the Allies in 1945.

Dr. Hegeman said the bloody handkerchief that provided cells for cloning was taken from the dead Fuhrer's shirt pocket by an aide, who gave it to the Soviets as proof that Hitler had died.

The expert was vague when asked to pinpoint where the Soviets are housing the clones. He did say that they are all incarcerated in a single military installation.

The chance that one or more of them might escape exists, he added, but "are quite remote."

"Even if a Hitler did get away there is no way he could rise to such heights as the original," he said. "Today's masses would probably laugh in his face."

— HENRY WEBER

'I know,' says eyewitness, 'I helped them do it!'

POLICE SAY...

Man beat mom to death for having snake in her belly

A 43-year-old man beat his mother to death because he thought she had a snake in her belly and he wanted to kill it!

James Arthur allegedly told cops in Bloomington, Ind., that he was fighting the snake when it fled into 67-year-old Mabel Arthur's body, leaving him no recourse but to attack her in order to kill it.

He was charged with murder, authorities said.

83-year-old woman is four months pregnant!

WEEKLY WORLD 55¢

NEWS

YOUR CHINESE HOROSCOPE
See what's in store for
you in the next 12 months!

April 12, 1988   30587   VOL. 9, Issue 27

Skeletons hailed as discovery of the century

ADAM AND EVE FOUND IN ASIA

Roly-poly
pet owner
barbecues her
husband's parrot —
for making fat jokes

* * *

**Priest exorcises
car possessed by
spirit of Satan**

* * *

**DINOSAURS HONKED LIKE
BUICKS, SAYS EXPERT**

* * *

**Transplant stunner! Mom gives
her legs to crippled daughter**

. . . and she was a
space alien,
say shocked
scientists

150

OVERPOWERING EVIDENCE! Dr. Bengt Naslund's discovery sheds new light on the origin of the human race. The famed archaeologist claims we are all descendants of a caveman father and a mom from a distant planet. Below, an artist's sketch of Adam and Eve.

IS THIS ADAM & EVE?

By HENRY WEBER

A leading scientist claims to have found the remains of Adam and Eve — remains that prove Adam was a caveman and Eve was a beautiful space alien!

"The evidence is overpowering," Dr. Bengt Naslund told reporters in Malmo, Sweden. "A Neanderthal man and extraterrestrial woman were father and mother of the human race as we know it.

"We are all descendants of an inter-species union and can trace at least half of our genetic heritage to outer space."

The archaeologist's claim, though fantastic, is based on evidence unearthed during a five-year dig in the hills north of Bayburt, Turkey.

After decades of research he satisfied himself that the Garden of Eden had been located in the region. And the discovery of skeletal remains late last year convinced him that he had found it.

"Finding the probable site of Eden was quite a coup but it paled in comparison to the skeletons themselves," said the expert.

"They were less than 40 yards apart and were obviously covered up in the same landslide that buried Eden. But there were glaring differences in their structures.

"The male was Neanderthal, short and powerfully built with the high cheekbones and sloping forehead that characterized Neanderthals.

"But the female was unlike anything I've ever seen. Long, weak bones tell me that she was long-legged and willowy, with delicate facial features and greater brain capacity than women have today.

"To say that she came from another planet requires very little imagination.

"This woman had none of the attributes that would have equipped her for survival on Earth at that time.

"There is no doubt that she was the product of evolution in a less hostile environment. All she had going for her was a mind."

Analysis of bones and organic matter taken from the site indicate that the man and woman lived and died about 60,000 years ago, said Dr. Naslund. That coincides with an unexplained leap in human intelligence and the emergence of modern man, two evolutionary steps that have never been adequately explained, he said.

"We can only conclude that a super-evolved Eve brought intelligence to the genetic pool and gave birth to modern men," said the expert.

"Naturally our study is only beginning. We must find out who or what Eve really was — and if possible, where she came from."

Garden of Eden site yields bones from 60,000 years ago

2 teens die in Russian roulette club

Two teens who shot themselves to death may have died proving how macho they were — as members of a Russian roulette club.

The bodies of Richard Aloy, 18, and Jose Peraza, 16, were found in the same house on different days.

Both boys had died from gunshot wounds to the head.

Police investigating the Homestead, Fla., shootings were told by a friend of the victims that a group of teenagers in the town often played Russian roulette together.

WEEKLY WORLD NEWS
April 12, 1988

3

151

BIGGER!

Sneezing makes your bust

By BEATRICE DEXTER

An allergy specialist has come up with some startling news for women — sneezing increases the bustline.

Dr. Arturo Magrini, an allergist in Milan, Italy, studied 800 women with long-term allergies and found that those who had endured more than five years of symptoms showed a slight, but significant, enlargement of the bust.

The controversial findings have been disputed by some experts, but Dr. Magrini says his careful calculations during the study provide proof positive of his findings.

Bra sizes of 800 in study increased, says doc

"After a good many years of strenuous blowing and sneezing, all the women I studied very definitely grew larger around the bust," Magrini said in a letter to the *Immunology Journal*. "Most increased at least one bra size, but several increased as much as three bra sizes — from an A cup to a D cup.

"I took all other variables into account, and my findings were quite clear. The action of sneezing without a doubt does influence bust size."

Magrini theorizes that sneezing develops the chest muscles and this influences breast size. He also believes that long-term fluid retention in the lungs experienced by most allergy sufferers may result in larger measurements after a number of years.

His ideas have excited much interest among colleagues, and some skepticism.

"Dr. Magrini is a serious scientist and I have no doubt that he believes what he's saying," said one allergist, Dr. Guiseppe Loango of the University of Milan. "But these findings would have to be checked and rechecked before I would be convinced."

Others back Magrini's findings, however, pointing out that chest measurements do increase following regular exercise of the chest muscles and sneezing would be considered exercise.

"Most women did not notice the change in their bust size or attributed it to other factors," Magrini wrote.

"But some realized what had happened and actually avoided treatment of their underlying allergic problem so that breast augmentation would continue."

Magrini cautioned colleagues to be alert to allergy patients who were suffering through their sneezing for purposes of increasing their bust size.

"We must convince these women to undergo treatment for their allergies and turn to plastic surgery if they wish to be bustier," he said.

152

What's for dinner? Worms and maggots!

Yum-yum!

By JACK ALEXANDER

Weirdo Welshman Dai Morgan would pass up a juicy steak any time for scrumptious mouthfuls of his favorite foods — slimy little worms and maggots.

And the burly, 210-pound rugby player doesn't mind if his meals are still alive when he sits down to eat.

"They wriggle when I cram them in, but they don't have a chance once I've chewed and crunched them up," said Morgan, 31.

Man hopes wacky diet will get him into record books

MAGGOTS like these are a gourmet treat for Morgan.

Dirty Dai didn't know what a tasty treat he was missing until he got bored during a rugby match in his hometown of Pyle, Wales.

"I picked up a worm and swallowed it," he said. "It was a bit earthy but went down real good. And I've been slurping worms ever since."

When Dai gets a craving for the creepy crawlers, his teammates and his girlfriend, Margaret, are willing to let him eat alone.

His queazy pals sneaked off the playing field one day when Dai started digging in the ground for a snack.

"I found a nice juicy one near the goal line," he said. "I prefer eating huge handfuls which you actually get your teeth into, but some of them escape by slithering down my chin."

The brawny bachelor's bizarre meals often include live maggots — pints and pints of the filthy creatures.

"I have trouble getting enough of them because other guys on the team are pretty keen on them, too," said Dai.

But the wacky Welshman aspires to a much higher goal where worms are concerned.

He dreams of being the world's champ worm eater.

"My main aim is to get the record for worm eating. I reckon I could eat 30 or 40 of 'em at a sitting," said Dai.

BRAWNY bachelor Dai Morgan loves to chew down on a plate of wriggly worms.

Pit bull kills prize horse!

A pit bull was being held by animal control officers after a horse breeder claimed the dog had attacked and killed his 4-week-old prize filly — valued at $7,000 to $10,000!

The horrified breeder, Dick Schneible, said he found the filly, Sun Glow Maid, lying in the pasture near his home in Cocoa, Fla., with her nose chewed off.

Schneible said he spotted one of his neighbor's two pit bulls that was "solid red with blood." He took blood samples from the dead horse and the dog's hair to have them analyzed.

"If the blood samples match," Schneible said, "it's proof that the dog killed the horse."

Parents put romance on back burner when baby is born, says new study

Couples all but give up sex after the birth of a new baby. That's the word from *Parenting* magazine, which polled 6,000 readers and found:

● 64 percent have never spent a weekend away together without their babies.

● 82 percent of mothers and 77 percent of fathers agree that sex life suffers after couples become parents.

● 78 percent agree that the frequency of sexual intercourse decreases dramatically in the first six months after a baby is born. 49 percent say it's still down a year later.

WEEKLY WORLD NEWS (ISSN 0199-574X) Published weekly by Weekly World News, Inc., 600 S. East Coast Ave., Lantana, Fla 33462. MAIL SUBSCRIPTIONS $13.95 a year in U.S., $19.95 a year in Canada, $25.00 a year for foreign addresses. Second Class postage paid at Lake Worth, Fla., and at additional mailing offices. POSTMASTER: Send address changes to WEEKLY WORLD NEWS, 600 S. East Coast Ave, Lantana, Fla 33462

A space alien made me pregnant — then stole my baby!

Incredible account has been clearly proven, expert says

By HENRY WEBER

A saucer-eyed space alien got a New York woman pregnant and then returned to kidnap her baby in two of the most brazen close encounters on record!

That's the word from Temple University expert David Jacobs, who says 30-year-old Christine Florenz's mind-boggling experiences have been confirmed in interviews conducted under hypnosis.

"Her experiences couldn't be a hoax because we gathered our information when she was in a deep hypnotic trance," said Jacobs.

"There is no way she is lying. Over the past 20 years we have studied over 500 cases of alien abductions and we are certain the extraterrestrials are here."

Miss Florenz knows that all too well — and wishes she didn't. She says 3-foot aliens plucked her from the backseat of her mother's car in 1985 and used strange medical instruments to impregnate her aboard their spaceship.

"It all started when I was making a car trip with my mother and sister," said Miss Florenz. "Eventually we arrived at our destination three

CHRISTINE FLORENZ

no way we could account for the lost time.

"I was very worried and went to see a doctor who suggested he should hypnotize me to help work out what was wrong.

"When he played back the tape of our session I was terrified to learn that I had been taken away in a giant silver spaceship and subjected to horrible sexual acts.

"But the real horror didn't hit until I found out I was pregnant. I had actually been made pregnant by an alien. I

was going to have an alien's baby."

An alien, she said, that had huge black eyes and only three fingers on each hand.

"They had a human form but were only 3½ feet tall with slightly larger than normal heads, huge black eyes and small pointed chins," she continued.

"All they had for mouths were tiny slits. And they didn't have noses, ears or hair. As I was laying there watching them I was completely helpless. They seemed to be

controlling all my movements with their minds.

"One of them put a strange metal contraption on my arm and leg. Then they started prodding me all over with strange instruments and I passed out."

When Miss Florenz awoke, she was back in her car with her mother and sister — none of them aware that anything extraordinary had happened.

Two months later Miss Florenz learned that she was pregnant and decided to have an abortion. But doctors at the

abortion clinic told her she wasn't pregnant at all.

The doctors who diagnosed her pregnancy earlier were baffled, she added.

"They insisted that I had been pregnant but they couldn't explain what happened to my baby," she said, although it's all but obvious that the aliens who got her pregnant returned for the unborn child.

Tragically for Miss Florenz, the alien fetus' ultimate fate is not — and may never be — known.

Preacher hides 32 years in coal mine

Preacher Josef Nebl and his wife think the world ended in 1956 and they've been living in a coal mine — afraid to come out — ever since!

"We tried to convince them that the world has not ended but they won't listen to reason," Police Capt. Oldrich Dankova told reporters in Ostrava, Czechoslovakia.

"The old man called us agents of the devil. He said he won't leave the mine until the Lord commands him and told cops that the minister became obsessed with the idea that the world was headed for a nuclear holocaust and advised his flock to prepare for the end on May 1, 1956.

The Nebls' doomsday saga came to the attention of authorities after a couple of eyed preacher standing at the schoolboys spotted the wild-entrance to the mine last December.

Investigation revealed that both now 80, shut down their Rev. Nebl and wife Karel, fire-and-brimstone church and moved underground into the

By HENRY WEBER

mine 32 years ago — on March 30, 1956.

Stanislav Brand is a former member of Rev. Nebl's fundamentalist congregation. He said he

"He cracked like an egg," said Brand, who was once one of the preacher's closest friends. "It got to the point that his sermons were totally irrational.

"He wanted all of us to join him in his holocaust shelter, which has a spring for water

and enough non-perishable food to last a lifetime.

"When nobody would heed his call he got even more set in his ways. In the end he believed that God was going to wipe out everyone but Karel and him.

"He thought they would be the new Adam and Eve."

Police now doubt that Mrs. Nebl is alive.

"In our limited conversa-

tions with Rev. Nebl he has refused to answer questions about his wife and she has not spoken for herself," said Del. Dankova.

"Of course, we'll never know if she's alive or not. Rev. Nebl has cut off communica-

tions with us and all contact depends on him.

"There are miles of tunnel down there and he knows them better than any man alive.

"The old man could elude us for years."

Dead body explodes in funeral home as family looks on, suit says

CORPSE BLOWS A CASKET!

By PETE COOKE

Family members who gathered at a Texas funeral home to mourn the death of 38-year-old Robert Cavazos Jr. reeled in horror when the dead man's corpse suddenly exploded, according to their shocking lawsuit.

The force of the blast ripped open Cavazos' cement-lined coffin and filled the funeral home in Raymondville, Tex., with "a horrendous, foul odor," according to Maria Perez, the family's attorney.

The lawyer said Cavazos' body exploded because it was not embalmed and gases formed within the corpse as the de-

composition process occurred. The room with the casket when they

'Robert's 82-year-old mother, Theresa, and about 20 mourners were at the funeral home on a Sunday morning in a

Cadaver's kaboom sparks $500G suit, says lawyer

heard a loud explosion and smelled a real foul stench," Miss Perez told *The NEWS*.

"They could see the body through the cracked casket and saw that Robert had been buried in his under-wear," Miss Perez said. "They still have night-mares!"

The family's anguishing experience began when Cavazos, who was divorced and lived with his mother, died of natural causes in his sleep. Cavazos' elderly mom and

18-year-old son were in the room when employees of Duddleston Funeral Home came for the body of the six-foot-four, 380-pound man.

"James Duddleston said they couldn't get their gurney through the doorway, so he called in some police officers, firemen and two police officers," Miss Perez said.

According to Miss Perez, the family was later told by

put two blankets on the floor, then rolled the body out of bed and dumped it onto the floor. They grabbed the blankets and held his arms and dragged him through the house as his mother and son watched. It was highly offensive."

"They the family the family

SHATTERED FAMILY: The dead man's brother Juan, center, his son Robert and his mother Theresa.

funeral home officials that body and casket onto the "embalming Robert wouldn't back of a flatbed truck for do any good because he was the ride to the cemetery. Miss so large and they could also Perez said. save $120 that way."

Several hours after Cavazos' corpse exploded mourners stood in front of Duddleston Funeral Home watching in disbelief as workers used a crane to hoist the dead man's

The attorney filed a lawsuit on behalf of the Cavazos family demanding $500,000 in damages.

Funeral parlor officials have denied any negligence in the case.

Housewife tells of bizarre encounter with low-flying spacecraft

UFO knocked my fillings loose!

By HENRY WEBER

I thought my head was going to explode, says horrified gal

A low-flying UFO caused such a tremendous change in air pressure that Shelley Mclenaghan's tooth fillings popped right out of her mouth!

"The pressure was so great I thought my head was going to explode," said the 29-year-old woman from Bolton, England.

"It was terrifying," she added. "My teeth were vibrating and when I tried to run away it was like being in a nightmare.

"My legs and arms moved, but in slow motion. I tried to scream, but nothing came out.

"Finally everything went hazy.

"The next thing I remember is bursting through the side door at home."

The young woman's chilling encounter with the saucer-shaped starship happened in 1976.

But her emotional scars were so deep that only now is she able to talk about it. And she says it has chang-

ed her life forever. "Every-thing is so uncertain now," she said. "I desperately want children. But in a world where something so frighten-ing as this can happen, I'm afraid to have them."

Mrs. Mclenaghan was just a girl of 17 when the eerie star-ship flew overhead. She says she had just gotten off a bus and was walking home when lights appeared in the sky.

"The lights were about four

or five times the size of a star and I thought to myself that in my mouth. Somehow I was they were, well, weird," she said.

"Then the lights merged and a real nuts-and-bolts craft zoomed right at me. It was the size of a house, flat on top, with sloping sides, a trap door and tripod legs.

"It was spinning on an axis," she continued. "Sud-denly it tilted toward me. Then there was a terrible pressure in my head and

shoulders and a funny taste in my mouth. Somehow I was able to run away and get home.

"I was so shaken that my mother thought I had been raped."

The young woman reported the incident to the authori-ties.

But they treated it like a joke in spite of the fact that a dentist confirmed the fill-ings had literally crumbled in her mouth.

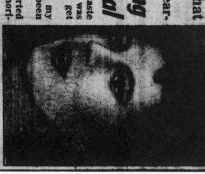

ALIEN starship flew so close to housewife Shelley Mclenaghan, shown above in an artist's sketch, that it dis-lodged her tooth fillings.

D1135856